The Flowers of Hiroshima

EDITA MORRIS

Marzani & Munsell, Inc.

NEW YORK · MCMLX

for Ira

The Flowers of Hiroshima

BOOKS BY EDITA MORRIS

Birth of an Old Lady and Other Stories
My Darling from the Lions
Three Who Loved
Charade
Echo in Asia
The Flowers of Hiroshima

The Flowers of Hiroshima

One

Heavens! Already five o'clock. How time flies! I'll
never get the *fusuma* put up, or the bedcover stitched,
before our new lodger returns. Yet I don't want to dis-
appoint that nice young man. If he likes it here,
mightn't he recommend us to his acquaintances in
Tokyo? Perhaps—perhaps better times are on the way.
(Dear Mrs. Bullfinch, don't sing so loudly in your
cage! You distract me, you drive me out of my mind,
darling.)

I wonder, will our American guest hate a pillow stuffed with rice? Will he dislike a bed no higher than the floor? Well, dislike it or not, he'll have to put up with it. Now I must get on with my cover, and no more delays. It's striking material—spinach green with a design of orange-colored branches. Dashingly modern!

How pleasant it is to kneel on the floor, stitching away, while the tea water bubbles on the brazier beside me. I love my little house, love to toil for my home, for my husband, for my gay fat children, my thin young sister. With a lodger to look after as well, I'll be working from sunrise till moonrise.

But to think that my young sister came close to losing us this precious guest! (Oh, what is it, Mrs. Bullfinch? I just gave you a lettuce leaf. You pushed it out of your cage, did you? *Bad* Mrs. Bullfinch! Wait. I'll pick it up for you. It's lucky I'm so light on my feet, isn't it? I spring up, I kneel down, I spring up, I kneel down, a hundred times a day. Well, here's your leaf. Now let me sew in peace, will you?)

Where was I in my thought? Oh yes, I was thinking of my American lodger and Ohatsu. We were standing beside our bamboo gate chatting, small sister and I, when this tall boy with the tousled fair hair, wearing a blue shirt and a sports jacket, stopped to ask his way. His eyes, as blue as his shirt, were nice. He had a nice voice too. He didn't shout when he talked, as most foreigners do. It was my sister who was impolite.

"Your shoe's almost on foots of glasshopper, sir!"

She smiled, as she said it, I'm glad to say. But she was trembling with rage (Ohatsu *hates* Westerners) as she snatched up the green insect and ran with it toward the house.

To make up for my sister's discourtesy, I offered the young foreigner my help in my best English. "Perhaps I could direct you, sir?"

But he had eyes only for Ohatsu. Apart from being tall as a tree, he had a neck like a giraffe's, which came in very handy just then, I must say. He stretched that long neck, staring after beautiful Ohatsu, who was running across our garden in her long, flying kimono.

"Please excuse my young sister. She's so fond of—of grasshoppers." That didn't sound right, I knew, but how could I explain to a stranger, an American to boot, the reason why Ohatsu's so deeply in love with everything that's alive, grasshoppers included?

[5]

"Gosh, is she your sister? She sure is good-looking!" the foreigner said.

Then the blood came to his cheeks; no doubt he thought he'd said something wrong. He looked surprised when I burst out giggling. The whole incident was so comic—the green, kicking grasshopper, the blushing foreigner, the raging Ohatsu. Remembering my manners, I clapped my hand over my mouth and almost at once I had control of myself.

"Look, I dumped my suitcase at the New Hiroshima Hotel, but damned if I can find the place again," the foreigner explained. "Holy smoke! How you find your way around this town beats me."

Again I had to choke back a giggle. For I was fashioned by nature to laugh; I have a round face, an upward-curving mouth, two dimples in my cheeks. Almost anything can strike me as funny, even an odd expression like "Holy smoke!" and the way foreigners keep getting lost in our country, where the streets have no names, nor the houses numbers. The young American seemed to find that funny too.

"I spent more time hunting for addresses in Tokyo than I did attending to business," he told me with his open smile. Then he blushed again, perhaps because he felt he had criticized my country. How delicate he must be inside, in spite of his size, how finely spun the fibers of his heart! I hastened to reassure him.

"I've been in Tokyo too. I know what you mean, sir."

"You do? Then give me a clue how to find places."

(Oh, tea water, tea water, *must* you boil over just now? I hate being disturbed when I'm going over, word for word, step by step, what I've done during the day. There, I have lifted you off the red-hot coals. Now why are you grumbling inside your pot-belly? Why does your wicked spout pour scalding water over my hand? Let me go on sewing his bedcover, please!)

But I've lost my train of thought. Well, never mind. The long and short of it is that the young foreigner decided to give up his room at the hotel and lodge with us (after I had told him, ever so subtly, that I had a room to let), and I felt so lighthearted at the thought of the extra *yen* I'd be earning that I went off into laughter again.

We stood chatting pleasantly together, and in a few moments I had learned all about this young man. He is in Japan on business for a shipping firm in Seattle. It seems his stepfather is part owner of this company, and that's how the young man "wangled" (funny word!) the opportunity to come here, he said. For years and years he's been dreaming of visiting Japan.

"I knew this Japanese girl once—back in Seattle," he confided to me. "Her name was Tosho Hamada. She was the best-looking girl in our high school."

As he spoke, the young American could not keep his eyes away from the *shojii* of our house, behind which Ohatsu had disappeared. Quickly I put two and two together. Ohatsu—Tosho Hamada. So that's why he was so willing to give up staying in the fine New Hiroshima Hotel!

"This girl, this Tosho Hamada, I never knew her really well. But I guess I'll always remember her. I was only a kid, but I must have been sort of in love with her. Why, I even used to write poems to her!" He grinned that nice grin of his. "When I was up in Tokyo I didn't see any girls like her, though I looked, plenty. I mean, some of those Tokyo girls are good-looking, all right, but somehow . . ."

The American gazed at our tranquil garden, with its

single cherry tree by the sleeping pond. Perhaps he was thinking that Tosho Hamada's garden looked like that. "Gosh, it's going to be swell staying here with you," he burst out.

I smiled and put up my hand to smooth my hair, then regretted the impulsive gesture. My kimono sleeve had slipped back and for a moment my bare arm was exposed. Dear me, I thought, did the foreigner see my scars? But as good luck would have it, someone shouted my name at that moment.

"Yuka! Yuka-san!"

"Excuse me, sir."

"Look, Sam is my name. Sam Willoughby—but that's too difficult. Just call me Sam."

"Thank you, sir. Now I must go."

Old Mrs. Nakano down the street was still calling me, and the foreigner and I looked around. How strange! Suddenly I saw Nakano-san with *his* eyes. I love Nakano-san and the other old lady who shares her shack, but as I gazed at them through the eyes of this Westerner I realized how rusty, how ashen, they look. They really look miserable, like so many Hiroshima survivors.

"I always take my two neighbors to the toilet at this hour of the evening—that is to say, to an empty field," I told the young American, who quickly looked away. (How peculiar are the reactions of foreigners!)

"Look . . ." he began, and then broke off, for Ohatsu had drifted back into our handkerchief of a garden. Gently she seated herself on the bench beneath our cherry tree.

"Guess I'll shove off now and go pick up my bag," the foreigner announced. "Will it be okay if I come back about five?"

"Any time will be 'okay,'" I replied.

"Yuka! Yuka!" shouted Nakano-san.

"Oh, now I must run! But everything will be ready for you at five. I'll have the *fusuma* put up and . . ."

"*Fusuma?*"

But I was certainly not going to tell my precious lodger-to-be that our house has only two small rooms, one of which I meant to divide into two with the help of a sliding panel. There are many things I don't intend our visitor to find out, things that would stop him from sending us other lodgers. Oh, I must use all my cleverness and tact, when he comes, to keep him from—from guessing what kind of family he's staying with.

Bowing quickly to him, I set off as fast as I could in my long kimono, taking care not to stumble into any of the deep holes that dot our street, which is as narrow and twisting as a chewed-up string. I wondered as I hurried along whether the young foreigner would be able to get used to lodging in this back alley. Would the screaming of children deafen him, I thought, and the shouts of their mothers, calling from house to rickety house? How would he react to the smells, and to our spitting, clawing alley cats? Tripping over a mound of rotting fish, I all but fell into a puddle of water before reaching Nakano-san and old Tamura-san. They grasped my arms, and the three of us set off toward the empty lot.

I turned my head as we went, and saw the young American staring after us, his eyes narrowed with amazement. His gaze was focused on the heads of my two friends—and small wonder. For Nakano-san and Tamura-san don't own a hair between them! Not a single hair. Pressing their chilly old arms to my warm body (I love them so!), I sent him a smile as our little trio trotted around the corner of the street.

Done! The last stitch taken. Oh, what's wrong now, Mrs. Bullfinch? A caraway seed? Wait, I'll give you one. I hear long steps outside—long, determined Western steps, not the light clacking of Japanese *getas*. It's my lodger. Quick, Mrs. Bullfinch, snatch your caraway seed, darling. Don't stand on ceremony. Dear me! I haven't put up that *fusuma* yet.

Two

"The young American is going to spend a couple of days with us, small sister."

That was how I broke the news, and Ohatsu was furious. Not that she said anything, of course. That would have been unthinkable for a younger sister. But she blew up her cheeks like balloons, as angry children do, and she kept her breath inside her face as I spoke to her. (Well, that's better than blowing it out, isn't it? Especially if harsh words would have flown out at the same time.)

"You will be nice to him, Ohatsu, won't you?" I went on. "If he likes it here, he might recommend us to other foreigners. You'll entertain him in the garden after supper, won't you?"

"I don't like haro-sans, elder sister."

"I wish you wouldn't use that stupid expression," I admonished her. But then I had to smile, for the fact is that I too always think of Americans as "haro-sans." It's silly; all those words that came in after the war are silly. Just because Americans always say "hello" is no reason to call them hello-sans—or haro-sans, since we Japanese always mix up our "l's" and "r's." "Anyway, whether you like them or not, I expect you to be nice to him," I told Ohatsu.

"I will, elder sister," she answered quietly, bringing tears of shame to my eyes. For of course Ohatsu realizes that I am using her beauty as bait. If we didn't adore each other, she'd hate me for it.

Well, that unpleasant moment is over, and now I sit on the floor, sewing peacefully, while outside on the garden bench Ohatsu chats with our lodger. It's deep night, but the tender light from our stone lantern bathes their faces. And on the wooden table stands my little pitcher of saké. Carefully Ohatsu fills Sam-san's cup.

"*Dozo.*" Each time she refills his cup, she whispers her "please," bowing from her slender waist. Oh, small sister's voice is as silken as the snoring of my bullfinch, sleeping in the wicker cage beside me.

Through a crack in the *shojii* I can see our lodger gazing at her in delight. (What nice things *shojiis* are! It's a great help in life that they slide open and shut so noiselessly.) Sam-san sighs.

"Why you sigh, prease?" asks Ohatsu worriedly, and I hope that this young haro-san won't laugh at her pronunciation.

"Was I sighing? We-l-l-l, that was just with contentment," says our lodger. His voice is warm and candid—the clue, I think, to his whole nature. "You know, I'm going to hate leaving here," he tells her. "Just going to hate leaving Japan."

"Why, prease? Like Japan betterer than America?"

"Better than America?" He raises his blond eyebrows. "Are you kidding? No, it's just that—well, my life's fallen into a kind of pattern back home. A pattern I don't much like."

Our lodger stops, and I'm surprised at the tense expression around his mouth. It doesn't go with his smooth forehead and the dreamy look in his eyes, set so far apart. When he goes on, his voice sounds edgy.

"This job I've got with the shipping firm—well, it's not my kind of job. To tell the truth, my stepfather talked me into taking it. My own father was a doctor. He had a country practice outside Seattle."

"Have to work hard in slipping firm? Have to do *arubeit* often?" Ohatsu asks politely.

"*Arubeit?*"

"Yes—mean extra work in evening, like all have to do in Japan. Come from German word, *arbeit*."

"Gosh, no!" Sam-san laughs then. "No *arubeit* for me, after the daily grind."

"So study in evening?" Ohatsu asks.

"Not on your life!" The young American seems outraged at the suggestion. "I try to have *fun*. If the weather's nice, for instance, I take my car, or go with one of the other fellows, and we drive around."

"Drive where?"

"Where? Oh, no place in particular. Just around. Sometimes we'll take in a movie, stop and have a couple of beers. Maybe we'll go pick up some girls . . ."

Through the crack in the *shojii* I can see that Ohatsu is looking bewildered. No wonder! I am bewildered too. The haro-san must have noticed this, for he gives up trying to explain how Westerners amuse themselves and asks Ohatsu what she does with *her* evenings. When she answers that she has a job as a telephone operator which keeps her busy most evenings, it's the haro-san's turn to look perplexed.

"Why, you don't look husky enough to work such long hours." He peers at Ohatsu. "In fact, you know what you look like? Like a little ghost, in that white kimono, with those white flowers in your hands."

"Ghost?" Ohatsu gazes down at the pansies she's just picked in our garden. (Oh, too bad! Small sister can't bear references to ghosts or to anything having to do with death.) "What do you mean, prease?" she asks in a shaking voice.

"Oh, just that you're so thin and pale—sort of ethereal, like a ghost," our lodger explains, and I see Ohatsu smile at him brightly in the starlight. (How she must

loathe the young man, to smile at him so charmingly!)
The haro-san mistakes her hatred for friendliness. He
moves closer to her on the bench.

"You know, Ohatsu-san," he says a little flirtatiously,
"you certainly have a lovely name. Are many Japanese
girls called Ohatsu?"

Small sister explains to him that the legendary Ohatsu, whose namesake she is, committed suicide for the
sake of love. Because of that romantic act, she has been
honored through the centuries.

"Killed herself for love? Well, if that isn't Japanese!"
the haro-san exclaims. "Ohatsu-san, would *you* do that?
Would you kill yourself for love?"

"Oh, I would! I would!" cries small sister passionately.

Dear me! I press my forehead to the crack in the
shojii and note Ohatsu's exalted expression. What can
have happened to her? She looks like a young girl in
love. But no, she is *ready* for love, that's all. She's as
eager to give herself as a plum is eager to be picked on
a morning in September. I draw in my breath, alarmed,
and at the same time elated.

But no doubt the haro-san thinks that all this is only coquetry. I see him reach out a finger, lifting the chin of a white pansy in Ohatsu's bouquet. He looks the flower deep in its expressive face and asks softly, "Would you give me that flower, Ohatsu-san—to remember you by?"

What a mistake! Small sister stares at our lodger, as horrified as if he had fingered her own red heart instead of the pansy's petal. Snatching the bouquet away from him, she presses it to her breast. She jumps to her feet (I too get to mine) and comes dashing into the house, colliding with me in the dark.

"Ohatsu!"

"Let me be, elder sister!" Ohatsu cries. She runs to the wall closet, pulls out her bedding, flings it on the floor, and crawls, sobbing, beneath her *futon*.

What to do? When at a loss, says Aunt Matsui, that clever old lady, bring out more saké. It has saved countless situations and will no doubt save many more, to the end of time.

I snatch a fresh pitcher of saké from the hot water and go into the garden. As I place the pitcher on the

table (smiling, although I've burned my fingers painfully) I murmur a commonplace, slowly and politely,
as Aunt Matsui has taught me to do with honored
guests—honored men in particular. "Don't you love
the sound of crickets chirping in the starlight?"

"Gosh, Yuka-san, is your sister sore at me?"

As far as the haro-san is concerned, I realize that the
sound of crickets might as well be the whirr of sewing
machines, and the starlight the glare of neon bulbs. I
have a most delicate situation on my hands, one I must
solve quickly or we might lose this precious lodger.

When one of my children is sulking, I stick a lolli-
pop into his mouth, so now I thrust a cup of saké into
the haro-san's hand. He drinks it automatically, as one
drinks anything one's been offered, and I instantly refill
his cup.

"Small sister's terribly high-strung. You mustn't
mind her," I say.

"Mind her? How could I possibly *mind* her!" The
haro-san shakes his head. "Hell's bells, I must have offended her somehow. It was when I touched those
flowers . . ."

Our lodger is turning things over in his mind, and a frown wrinkles his forehead.

"No, no, don't worry," I break in, terrified he might ask about Ohatsu's bouquet. "Ohatsu had to go to bed, that's all. You see, in Japan everyone gets up at dawn because he has to do more than one job in order to—" (Dear me, I almost said, "in order to eat.") "—in order to make ends meet," I finish lamely.

"I know." The haro-san laughs. "*Arubeit!* Well, I guess it's lucky for me you need *arubeit*, otherwise you'd never have taken me in. I'm sure glad you did, or I'd be sitting around right now with a bunch of tourists in that fancy Western-style hotel. That's not what I'm looking for in Japan. I'm interested in *people*, see? Hell of a businessman I am!" Sam-san laughs again, but the tense expression around his mouth has come back.

He sits gazing into his saké cup, turning it around and around so that the pale rice wine swishes about, staring at the shimmering pagoda painted on the cup's bottom.

"My old man drove all over the countryside fourteen hours a day looking after sick people who as often as not couldn't pay him. He didn't much care. It was human beings that interested him. I guess that's why he liked being a doctor."

"Didn't *you* ever think of being a doctor?"

"You bet. I even got in a couple of years at med school. But then Dad died and—well, I guess too many of his patients *hadn't* paid him. When my mother married again, my stepfather offered me this desk job with his firm. It's okay. But gosh, sometimes I think I ought to have gone on, been a doctor, like Dad."

Sam-san's forehead wrinkles, but then he laughs and says, "Well, one good thing about the job, it got me to Japan! I'd have been fifty by the time I got here under my own steam. And it's just the way I'd imagined it— only more so."

Stretching out his long legs, he leans back on the bench. His gaze follows the curved roof of our house, rests on Ohatsu's bed of white pansies, then on our grandfatherly stone lantern glowing in the night.

"Yeah, this is just about it," he says softly. "That pond—the cherry tree. Everything's perfect. You know, I can't get it through my head that this is the place the atom bomb fell on fourteen years ago. You and Ohatsu were lucky girls, all right."

"Oh yes," I say, "we were terribly lucky."

Sam-san looks up quickly. Has he heard in my voice something that troubles him? But I am well trained. I am smiling as I lean toward him, and all that the haro-san can see in the light of the stars is the face of —a very lucky girl.

Three

How beautiful, those little fish, resting crossways on their cone of cooked rice! I've brought my husband his lunch box and, having taken off its lacquered lid, am kneeling on a strip of straw matting, admiring the tasteful arrangement. I have nothing else to do until Fumio finishes a conversation with his boss. (Through the window of the office I can see the two of them standing talking together.)

A garage is a dizzy place, noisy, smelly, and drafty, but if I close my eyes I can slide back into my own world; oblivious to my surroundings, I am ready to wait for hours if need be. It's nothing new to me. Sometimes I had to wait all day for Fumio after he was called into the army. Every Sunday while he was in training I would wait for him in the Hiroshima railway station, along with scores—no, hundreds—of other young war wives. It strikes me suddenly that I've spent more time *waiting* for Fumio than in actually enjoying his company. I remember . . .

"May I bring you a newspaper to read, Nakamura-san?"

It's the head mechanic, being nice to me, as always, but, bowing low, I tell Komako-san not to bother. Now what was I thinking? Oh yes, of the railway station, remembering how sorry for my Fumio I used to feel when I caught sight of him in his enormous army boots. They were so big that he could easily have got both feet into one of them. Quick tears used to form in my eyes. But then I'd burst out laughing, for that's my nature. To my question as to why he couldn't get another pair of boots, Fumio would answer, "The army doesn't fit boots to the foot; the foot must fit the boot." How we laughed! Then he would have to hurry back to the war.

Pong. Pong. Pong.

The clock on the garage wall has whirred and struck three times. What *can* those two men be talking about so long in Fumio's little office? Two freshly painted trucks are leaving the outer yard, but their owner, Fumio's boss, doesn't follow their splendid example. That fat chatterbox is wearing my husband to a frazzle with his jabber.

How pale Fumio looks! Is it my imagination that he looks more ashen today than yesterday? That he looked more wan yesterday than the day before? Oh, I mustn't get all knotted up inside, as I was during the war, when I kept having miscarriages. I could produce babies only when life became normal again—at least *seemed* to become normal. Once more anxiety grips my heart, and I turn worriedly to the head mechanic.

"Did my husband eat a good breakfast this morning, Komako-san? Did he drink all his bean soup?"

Komako-san, who is walking toward my husband's office with a sheaf of papers, stops, but he doesn't answer my question.

I send him a bright smile (one mustn't burden people with one's private troubles) and coax him a little.

[27]

"He did take *some* breakfast, didn't he? A little rice, some bean soup?"

Like the pendulum of the clock, Komako-san's head swings from side to side. "It's too noisy in the garage for the accountant-san to get a good night's sleep. That's the reason he has no appetite in the mornings."

The head mechanic speaks to me politely from behind his hand. Komako-san wears a Western-style leather jacket, he has an American cap on his head, but his manners are wholly Japanese. It is rather a relief. (I can't help feeling that our Japanese ways are superior, even though my friend who taught me English tried to explain that they're not *superior*, just different. It's idiotic to talk of superiority, said my friend, who has traveled.)

Komako-san bows low. "It's not for me to say," he goes on, still speaking with his hand politely before his mouth, "but the accountant-san shouldn't spend too many nights here in his office. I know there's much work to be got through. I know he can't work very fast nowadays. Still . . ."

Ah, if that were only true! I mean, that Fumio sleeps away from home because he has so much work. It isn't the truth, alas. My husband is a diligent and painstaking employee—what Japanese isn't?—but the reason he so often spends a night in his airless cubbyhole here isn't zeal. I know, though I'd rather die than admit this, that it's his ever-increasing inability to make love to me. It isn't *arubeit* that keeps him away nights, but rather this mysterious difficulty whose cause he doesn't want me to guess. Oh, what a sad plight the two of us are in. If only I didn't have such a loving body!

Ah! Fatty has come out at last. He's leaving. No! Now he's changed his mind. Pulling out more crumpled documents from his bulging briefcase, he goes back into my husband's office, and Fumio bows and smiles, bows and smiles, while surreptitiously wiping sweat from his hollow temples. We live in terror of his losing his job; that would be so great a calamity we don't dare contemplate it. And so my husband stands respectfully listening, and I close my eyes and prepare for another long wait.

These big shots always love to hold forth, to keep their subordinates on tenterhooks while they listen, enamored, to the sound of their own voices. The Japanese "brass" (I learned that word from American movies, and "big shot" too, come to think of it) kept Fumio standing at attention for four years. Then when my young husband landed his first job, in a bank, the bank manager did the same.

How rebellious I used to feel! I'd be boiling over inside as I waited meekly for Fumio outside the bank building. Like thousands of Japanese young men, Fumio hadn't been able to finish his studies, so was without the degree which would have admitted him to an honored profession like his father's. He's so typical of young Japan that hasn't had a chance, that's never had boots to fit its feet. Although my marriage to Fumio was arranged by the matchmaker, I love him deeply, and I marvel at his heroic acceptance of circumstances. He has a firm core of inner pride. That core makes Fumio the man he is.

I spring up from my kneeling position.

"A visitor, a haro-san, asking for you outside the garage," Komako-san tells me behind his hand.

"A *foreign* visitor?" I pretend surprise. Naturally I hadn't told Komako-san that I've taken a foreign lodger; it wouldn't look well in Hiroshima. And the fact that I've taken a lodger at all would show the head mechanic that I'm anticipating bad times. Komako-san might let the cat out of the bag to the boss, and then what would happen?

"Hi there, Yuka-san!"

The haro-san in person! I can never get used to his informality, but I mustn't let on that I'm shocked. In Italy, do as the citizens of their capital do, my friend who taught me English used to advise me. When associating with a young American, I must behave like a lady from New York. So, "Hello, Sam-san!" I cry.

"Just came from my appointment with Mr. Yamomoto," says the haro-san, wiping his forehead with his handkerchief. He's dressed in a neat seersucker suit today, and has even combed his hair. "Holy smoke!" he exclaims. "I sure wasn't cut out for a business career. And that smart cooky Yamomoto could tell it right away; he had the jump on me from the word go. Just like my stepfather back in Seattle—" He breaks off and looks around him, wanting to change the subject. "Say, they've got quite a collection of old heaps in this garage!" he cries gaily.

I giggle. It's wonderful to have someone that I can laugh with for a change!

"No, these cars won't win any races," I agree. "But you haven't seen the prize one yet. It lives in the yard, and we call it 'Venerable Duck.' You see, it *waddles*. Fumio's boss lets us use it for picnics and excursions sometimes." I have an idea and lose no time in bringing it out. Time is money, especially in this case. "Why don't you stay over Sunday and go with us to Miyajima? It's cherry-viewing day; everyone will be there."

But Sam-san shakes his head. "I'm afraid, you'll have to count me out. I've got a couple of other guys to see here, but after that I'll have nothing to keep me in Hiroshima. I'd like to do a little sightseeing in Nara and Kyoto before flying home."

"How nice!" I say, smiling brightly so as not to show my disappointment.

Fumio's boss, a huge man like a Sumo wrestler, lumbers past us, giving me a brief nod, Western fashion.

"My husband's free now. Come in his office and meet him," I say to the haro-san.

Fumio's office is really only a passageway, lit by a tiny window which gives onto the yard. Besides his camp bed, the room holds a mass of garage junk—piles of tires, coils of rope, gasoline cans—and at first, in the dimness, I don't see my husband. Ah, there he is! At the other end of his gloomy cubbyhole, beneath the slit of a window, Fumio is standing, looking at some object in his hand. What is it? A letter he's reading— some invoice that Fat One left?

Suddenly I clap my hand over my mouth. It isn't a bill or an account that Fumio is studying—it's his own neck! Holding a pocket mirror in his hand, he is gazing at the left side of his neck with such concentration that he doesn't even notice us in the doorway.

I give a little cough. Fumio swings around, and in that moment I see that his face is twisted with anxiety, that his eyes are wild. But right away he has himself in hand. (*Dear* Fumio, how proud I am of you!) As he greets our young lodger his face is as calm and pleasant as ever. I hand my husband his lunch box, which he puts down absent-mindedly on the table beside a case of spark plugs, and suddenly I want to get our lodger out of that room as soon as possible. It's too revealing —the hand-mirror, the unwanted lunch . . .

"Come, Sam-san, I want to show you Venerable Duck," I cry, happy that he's a foreigner, unsuspecting of sudden switches in the conversation. But I'm so upset that I forget all manners and walk out of the room ahead of the two young men.

The dust-covered old Buick is full of passengers. I lift the "driver" up in my arms and kiss his fat cheeks, then set him on the ground and give his head a little shove from behind, reminding him to perform his ceremonial bow.

"This is Tadeo, Sam-san. And that's his sister," I explain, nodding toward my little daughter in the back seat.

"De-light-ed," cries the haro-san, his gangly body performing a Japanese bow. "And the other half-dozen— yours too?"

"No, just friends."

We all laugh, my husband included, which breaks the ice between the two men. My little boy and girl— oh, they are the most wonderful children in the world, I'm sure of that!—are both wearing red kimonos with a gay Mickey Mouse design. Sam-san vaults into the seat of the car (like a cowboy into his saddle, in the movies —I love it!) and as he lands on the ripped old cushion a cloud of dust flies upward. He coughs and laughs. How gay it is!

[34]

I'm still laughing when . . . Oh, Fumio's gazing at his neck again! He has slid into the driver's seat, beside Sam-san, and is stealing glances in the windshield mirror, and once more his eyes look wild. The whole incident only occupies a second, but icy fingers squeeze my heart. I feel as though I were choking, and have to open my mouth for air.

"Let's have some fun!" It's the haro-san, and I don't know whether he's noticed nothing or—disturbing thought—noticed too much. "Come on, everyone," he cries, "we'll take a ride. If we're going to take in that cherry-viewing festival on Sunday, we'd better make sure this old wreck still runs."

He says it just like that—quite casually, without even a smile. Ah, how sensitive this young foreigner is, how tactful! He felt my need to have him stay on a little longer, yet pretends to have noticed nothing, that everything is as gay as I want him to believe. What a handsome gesture! I shall never forget it.

It all happens so quickly; it's again just as in the movies. I'm installed in the rear seat, and my husband is starting the old car almost before I know what's happening. The young haro-san leans out of Venerable

Duck, which is already waddling toward the street. "*Sayonara*, you kids!" he shouts, and waves.

The sun glitters on his tousled blond hair. How vibrant he is with life! The children, clustered around the head mechanic, wave back. Everyone waves. Even Mickey Mouse, on Tadeo's and Michiko's kimonos, is waving. That is why I chose Disney-san's lighthearted little mouse as a design for my children's kimonos—because life is not always so cheerful.

Four

Who could have guessed that I'd be given a sudden treat? Really, I don't deserve such an enchanting outing—and offered for no reason at all. I lean back comfortably on the dusty upholstery as our old "heap" bumps down the road. With Fumio at the wheel, we honk our way through the still-unpaved streets of rebuilt Hiroshima.

What a commotion there is at this midday hour! People are slipping out of their offices to snatch a bite to eat or hurrying back with their empty lunch boxes under their arms. There's a terrible bustle. As we turn a corner, we almost run down two young ladies tripping across the street. They giggle, scampering to safety, and I give them a friendly wave, while my envious eyes take in the smart material of their new spring kimonos. At that moment an uncomfortable thought slips into my mind, like a pebble that works itself into one's shoe. What will I wear next Sunday at the cherry-viewing festival at Miyajima?

Before I knew that Sam-san would be coming along, I'd thought vaguely of putting on the green Western dress that my friend who taught me English sent me from Tokyo. Such bad luck that it has short sleeves! My friend, Keiko, must have forgotten what I can never forget—those telltale scars on my arm. It would take away all my pleasure in the occasion if I disclosed the hateful blemishes which my kimono fortunately hides.

Sternly I force the problem from my mind, telling myself that my appearance doesn't matter, seeing that I am a woman of thirty-one, married, a mother. It's Ohatsu who counts, and I shall see to it that she looks lovely for the haro-san. I get an idea. Why not pawn my silver hairpins, buy material, and beg Fukuda-san, our seamstress, to do a rush job on a kimono for small sister? Fukuda-san's full of neighborly spirit, and I'm sure that she'll oblige.

"A penny for your thoughts, Yuka-san."

Sam-san's open face is smiling at me from the front seat, and I smile back, though of course without answering. Imagine ever divulging one's thoughts—for a penny or a million *yen!* As a child I used to blurt out whatever was on my mind, but before I was six my mama-san had taught me good manners. Which is better, I wonder—to come right out with things, Western fashion, or to keep them hidden? Blurting out one's feelings makes one lose face, but gulping them down can give one a terrible stomachache sometimes.

Has our motorized duck gone mad? It's waddling along so fast that we're actually overtaking a bicycle, and Fumio turns round to give me a discreet smile of triumph. Dear Fumio! As the sun flashes on his strong white teeth, he looks just as strong and healthy as Sam-san, and happily I tell myself that things are bound to turn out all right.

"Where are we headed?" the foreigner cries. "I

haven't seen anything of Hiroshima yet. That appointment kept me tied up the whole morning. The city seems to be all rebuilt, just like Tokyo." He peers about. "Wonderful job you people have done since the war."

"Oh yes," I say quickly. "Everything's rebuilt. Everything's new."

Whatever happens, I don't want the haro-san to realize that the old Hiroshima still survives. For ours is a town built on rubble, and the old population, burned and broken, still lives on in slum districts which few foreigners ever see.

Fumio doesn't know English, but he has grasped the meaning of Sam-san's words. Without turning his head, he points his thumb at the rear pocket of the car, and I fish out a dilapidated guidebook and begin reading from it.

" 'Hiroshima is situated on a delta, where the five arms of the river Otha empty into the Inland Sea of Japan.' Can you hear, Sam-san?" I shout above the din of the traffic.

"Get a megaphone, guide," he calls back.

" 'Before August sixth, nineteen forty-five, Hiroshima was a thriving seaport with a population of three hundred and sixty thousand. But on the morning of that day, the great city vanished from the face of the earth. . . .' "

Dear me! This role of guide is more than I'd bargained for. In the pamphlet it says that on August 6, in a single minute, between 8:15 and 8:16 A.M., sixty thousand of our city's homes were reduced to ashes and a hundred thousand people were burned or crushed to death. I *hate* statistics! Behind each digit human faces seem to stare at me in agony. I stop reading.

"It's so noisy I can't make you hear," I lie quickly. "You can have a look at this when we get home."

Well, thank goodness I got out of that! I slip the book back into the torn pocket, but before I have time to lean back in my seat we run into fresh trouble. We're driving past the Atom Bomb Museum now, in front of which two sightseeing buses are drawn up. Tourists with cameras are piling out to visit our gruesome collection of relics and photographs. And of all things, Sam-san, who doesn't understand what sort of "museum" this is, wants to stop and go inside.

I try to dissuade him. "You'd better come back in the morning. It's awfully crowded now."

But the haro-san looks put out, so there is nothing for it but to obey his wish, even though it may spoil our afternoon. After all, Sam-san is our honored guest, is he not?

"Stop, *dozo*, Fumio. Stop, please," I murmur in Japanese.

But instead of stopping, our Venerable Duck leaps forward. Fumio's foot is pressing down on the accelerator, and his face in the mirror looks grim. (Small wonder! Going into that museum is like visiting one's own grave, as one of us survivors said.) Rattling and swaying, our bird on wheels lumbers toward the river at breakneck speed. I have to gulp back a cry of fright. If my husband didn't disapprove of women's speaking up in Western style, I'd ask him kindly to slow down. As it is, I simply bite my lips and hold onto the seat.

A screech . . . a squeak . . . a squawk . . . Our old duck slithers and swerves, and, just before we reach the bridge—stops dead. We jump out.

"Some ride!" The haro-san laughs. He hurries toward the front of the car, but my husband has already raised the hood and is peering inside. He sends me an agonized glance. Take him away! is the entreaty I read in his eyes.

"Do you want to have a look at the river, Sam-san?" I inquire, and, without waiting for an answer, lead him toward the sloping bank. I slip and almost fall (on purpose) and go into peals of laughter to show that nothing is wrong. If Sam-san had been Japanese, he naturally would have interpreted my gaiety correctly and would have laughed louder than I. Instead, he throws a puzzled glance at Fumio, who is tinkering with the motor.

"I don't dig it!" he says. "What came over him anyway? What made him speed up like that? And why won't he let me help him?"

"Don't worry, Sam-san. It's nothing."

I keep up my pretense of gaiety almost automatically. Needless to say, Sam-san's first question can't be answered. As for the second, even an American should realize that Fumio has lost face. The car broke down because of his emotional driving, and now he feels mortified.

"Look! Aren't those girls on the river there pretty?"

I cry, for men, like children, forget everything the moment you dangle a new image before them.

The haro-san is still frowning, but as his glance goes to the rowboat his expression softens. Three girls, sweet as fresh leaves, are kneeling on the straw mats in the hull, and they are singing to the accompaniment of a *samisen*—such a sad little song.

"Why are they all dressed alike?" Sam-san asks me.

"Because they're orphans. That's the orphan asylum dress," I answer, wishing that my lodger wouldn't ask such embarrassing questions. But then so many things in Hiroshima are embarrassing for us!

"What's that bouquet of flowers doing down there in the river, Yuka-san?"

"Bouquet?" My face freezes. "Why, they're just some old flowers that someone threw in the water," I tell him, but Sam-san doesn't take his eyes away. He keeps staring at that bouquet of white pansies bobbing on a silvery wave, his chin jutting out stubbornly. It's an estimable quality, stubbornness, but what an unfortunate time to have it come to the fore.

"You're wrong," he announces at last. "That's a real bouquet! See, the stems are tied together with green cord!" The haro-san's chin juts out further. "I'll bet you anything someone put those flowers there—anchored the cord under that big stone."

He throws me a questioning glance, which I meet with a blank stare. The girls in their little boat are gliding by us, and as they catch sight of the floating bouquet the one who is rowing lifts her oars high so as not to disturb it. Little drops of water fall on the flowers, looking like shining tears. The girls lower their voices, and their chant grows sadder still.

"Hey!" my lodger cries suddenly. "What's the matter with Fumio?"

I swing about to see Fumio leaning limply against the open hood of the car. In frantic haste I climb the river bank.

"Fumio, what's the matter?" I cry. "Answer me!"

But our lodger has already reached Fumio, and has flung his arms about him with that Western decisiveness that I so admire. He makes him sit down on the runningboard of the old Buick.

"Here, take my handkerchief and go dip it in the river, Yuka-san. Hurry!"

Even as I clamber down the slope to wet the foreigner's huge handkerchief, I have time to admire him for the way he takes matters in hand. He has a real human sympathy for a fellow being in distress. But he's out of my mind in a second, and when I climb back toward the car I am trembling all over. Can this be it? The question beats at me. No, no! It's only the sudden May heat, only that Fumio wore himself out hammering at that wicked old engine.

"I tell you what. I bet it's a sunstroke," Sam-san says to me after we've helped Fumio into the back seat and are driving off, with the American at the wheel. "Yes sir, that midday sun of yours packs quite a wallop. I'm going to drive him straight to the hospital."

"Nie!"

Fumio must have understood the word "hospital," and he protests frantically. Of course it would be all over our neighborhood within the hour if Fumio were seen entering the hospital. Our evil landlord would hear about it at once, not to mention Fumio's boss. What would become of us then?

"Take us home, Sam-san," I say, squeezing my husband's icy fingers reassuringly.

"Not to the hospital? You sure?"

"No, home. Please, Sam-san."

"Okay. Home it is," says the haro-san, turning to see if Fumio is comfortable on the broken springs of the back seat. I see his eyes narrow, and I'm certain that he's saying to himself, "I don't dig it."

Ah, there are many things in Hiroshima that I don't want you to "dig," dear Sam-san! Suddenly I feel a hundred years older than you. You're so innocent; you haven't yet seen beyond our wall, beyond our defenses. For your sake I hope you'll leave Hiroshima knowing as little about what's behind that wall as everyone else.

five

What a lovely store, Fukuya's! What a lovely time we're having! I've been walking on air since we learned that Fumio's illness was just a touch of the sun, as Sam-san suggested, and nothing worse. Of course I didn't call in a doctor (people would have talked), but we did consult Hashimoto-san, the little medical student who lodges in our street, and this kind young man instantly agreed that Fumio must have had a slight sunstroke. My husband felt better at once, and has gone back to work. So now we're all happy as can be, and, taking the money I got for my silver hairpins, I have gone, with Sam-san, to Fukuya's department store to buy Ohatsu a spring outfit.

It is rare, one might even say it's unheard of, that I get a chance to shop. I'm far too poor. That's why I enjoy it so much, and again and again I catch our lodger watching me with a funny little smile. Perhaps I'm showing my delight too naïvely. Well, it can't be helped. Sam-san doesn't realize how few times in my life I've visited a large store. He doesn't know, either, that I have seen this very building with its interior filled with rubble, human bones mixed with the debris. As I gaze about me at the glittering counters, I feel him give my arm a squeeze. I smile up at him, and we set forth to conquer new worlds—this time the fascinating department where they sell inexpensive rayon goods.

"Hey—" begins Sam-san, and at this pet expression of his I get the giggles again.

"Hey, what?" I ask him mischievously.

"Will you tell me what Ohatsu needs with *two* under-kimonos? It's May. She'll roast to death."

I have to splutter. Still laughing, I explain the cause

of my unseemly mirth to the little group that has been following us about from counter to counter. They all giggle politely (behind their hands so as not to embarrass the foreigner), and I explain to my lodger that for centuries the girls of Japan have worn a series of under-kimonos, many more than two on occasion.

"In new, snappy countries like yours fashions can change overnight," I tell him. "Here it takes centuries. For instance, one of the under-kimonos must repeat the color used in the design of the top kimono—lilac, in this case."

"No siree!"

This "No siree!" comes not from Sam-san but from the assistant manager of the inexpensive-rayon department. He knows a little English, and has probably picked up that expression at the movies.

"Too bad, lilac big rage this spring," he explains. "Ladies cry, 'Lilac, lilac!' Inexpensive lilac rayon all gone." He taps his lovely gold teeth with his ball-point pen thoughtfully, smiles slyly. "Suggest mustard yellow instead. Got plenty of *that!*"

"Because nobody wants it?"

Dear me, why does the haro-san always blurt out

exactly what he's thinking? To prevent that stomach-ache one gets from keeping things back? But sales-men have thick hides—they'd starve to death other-wise—and the assistant manager of the inexpensive-rayon department flashes Sam-san a golden-toothed smile. He asks if the young lady for whom we're buy-ing this finery is the honorable foreigner's fiancee.

"I sure wish she were!" Sam-san says, laughing.

And how *I* wish she were. To have my frail plum-sprig of a sister taken care of by a fine, strong young man like Sam-san is my heart's desire. I can almost see the rivers of good red blood, with all their little side-streams, racing beneath the foreigner's healthy skin. Of course, Ohatsu would be furious with me for mar-rying her off to this foreigner in my thoughts! Gen-tle as she is, there's a great willfulness in small sister, a passionate desire to have her own way which fright-ens me at times. In her, as in so many Hiroshimans who have had too awful experiences in their childhood, hysteria is never more than a step away.

Now someone, a funny little man, steps forward and begins arguing with the assistant manager. This small, bent fellow in his country-bumpkin clothes, with his big wool cap pulled down over his head, has been following us from counter to counter for the last hour. In fact he has taken a greater interest in our purchases than we have. He begins complaining hotly to the assistant manager about that mustard-yellow material.

Heavens, the assistant manager is about to lose face! Somehow I must divert the farmer's attention. After all, the assistant manager is the second-in-command of the inexpensive-rayon department, a person of importance who has been devoting himself to us for at least ten minutes. Bowing, I ask the little peasant where he comes from, and he bows back, politely sucking in his breath, and informs me that he works on a silkworm farm outside Hiroshima. He has come to the city for a day's sightseeing, and as Fukuya's department store is new Hiroshima's super-attraction, he is spending his entire day there. But as soon as he caught sight of the haro-san, with his skyscraper body and fair hair, he concentrated his attention on him. He has attached himself to Sam-san as if the tall foreigner were an envelope, and he, the little silkworm farmer, a postage stamp.

"That mustard material," he tells me, coming stubbornly back to his argument, "don't buy it! It's the color of . . ."

The men in our little group smile broadly behind their hands, the women behind their new spring fans. "Say, what's the joke, Yuka-san? I hate to be left out of anything," complains the haro-san.

"It's something too rude to explain," I tell him.

Westerners, I have been told, have a peculiar mixture of prudishness and lewdness, which is why I don't translate the silkworm farmer's earthy joke. Sam-san's mind has already moved on to something else anyhow, in its impatient American way.

"Say, I just don't—"

"*Now* what don't you dig?" I nudge him jokingly, for of course that's his *most* favorite expression, and Sam-san grins down at me. He tells me that he can't understand why people are following us about from counter to counter. "They're sticking to us like burrs," he grumbles.

Three schoolgirls, holding hands, press close to us, and so does a young couple—newlyweds, to judge from their radiant looks. A stout woman who is fanning herself energetically touches our purchases with an inquisitive finger, while the little silkworm farmer is right beside us every second.

"There were only the school kids when we bought Ohatsu's sandals," Sam-san points out. "We picked up the newlyweds when we bought her sash, and we collected the others at the parasol counter. We've got an audience of eight people now, counting the salesman. Gosh, why don't they leave us alone?"

Over six feet tall, this young foreigner and without the sense of a little ladybird! Does he really expect me to scatter these people as one would scatter a flock of chickens, by clapping my hands? Japan's penniless shoppers have to buy with their eyes—doesn't the young American realize that? Humbly they take part in the shopping sprees of luckier people, and why shouldn't they?

"Hey! Is *he* crazy?"

The polite assistant manager is piling the packages into my arms, and the foreigner's eyebrows are raised in astonishment. Quickly I whisper to him not to interfere, and Sam-san shrugs his broad shoulders in mock despair.

"All right, *be* a beast of burden, if that's Japanese etiquette! Don't let me stop you." He shakes his head. "Where do we go from here?"

"Home," I answer, and how pleasant it is to say "home" to Sam-san! Oh, I know I mustn't feel this way. It's so new to me to have a gay, lighthearted companion, it has turned my silly head.

But Sam-san protests. "No, we're going to buy something for *you* now, Yuka-san."

"Yes, yes! Let us do so."

It's the newlyweds who say this; evidently they understand English. Once again Sam-san's eyebrows move up his forehead. He stares at them. Then a grin of understanding spreads across his face.

"I think I'm beginning to dig it!"

"Dig what?" I ask.

However, the young American isn't very expansive, as I have noticed before. He doesn't answer me, but his light-colored eyes move around our little group; then he nods slowly. Can it be that the meaning of our Japanese "neighborliness" is beginning to dawn on him? Perhaps something in it reminds him of the relationship his father, the country doctor, had with his patients, who sometimes could pay him only in gratitude and friendship.

The haro-san takes my arm. "Listen, how about getting you a pair of those hairpins, the kind that look like lollipops?"

"Oh, *buyens?*" My thoughts move from Sam-san to myself. I know it's not at all seemly for a married woman to accept gifts from a man, but dear me, I certainly would like some new *buyens* to wear at Miyajima! "That would be wonderful." I hear my imprudent voice. "You see, I sold my silver ones—"

I stop abruptly—too abruptly! Sam-san has smelled a rat, and I know from the way he looks at me that he's guessed how I raised the money for small sister's spring outfit.

"We'll do it another day," I cry, flustered. "We'd better go now; it's late."

But the haro-san doesn't budge. He keeps looking at me in a funny way, and I'm tortured with embarrassment. At last I move toward the escalators, with our whole little group in tow, and I've become so confused that I take the one going up instead of that going down. As I float skyward, I feel the sweetest pain in my breast. The escalator seems a gently moving bird on whose wings I'm soaring into a new and happier clime. Oh, it's vain, to be sure, but I do like the haro-san and enjoy the thought that he approves of me.

I jump off at the top. The others in our little group step off also, and they are all smiling warmly as they watch the young foreigner on the floor below, about to start up the moving stairs to join us. Meanwhile, our silkworm farmer stands at the bottom also, finger in mouth, gazing up at us like a little boy who has been left out of the fun. The country bumpkin has never seen a flight of stairs, much less an escalator, in his life. He's dying to climb on, but doesn't dare.

Dear me! With his Western impetuosity, my lodger grabs the silkworm farmer by his sleeve, showing him in sign-language how to put both his feet on the same step and to stand still while that creeping caterpillar carries him upward. The little man grins blissfully. The minute the bizarre pair—one tall as Mount Fuji, the other small and round as one of his own silkworm co-coons—reach the top, the farmer drags Sam-san to the down-going escalator. Then up they come again, and down they go. Our audience giggle happily behind their paper fans. Then they bow low to me and go their own ways.

And here come the haro-san and the silkworm farmer up the escalator again! This time the American joins me, while the bumpkin bows low to us several times, before dashing back to his beloved moving stairs. He has learned the trick now, and he'll be traveling up and down till the store closes at sundown.

"Say, quite a guy!" Sam-san says, laughing. "But what do you suppose happened to his head? Did you notice anything, Yuka-san—under that wool cap, I mean?"

We're walking toward the novelty department, and in that hurrying crowd it's easy to pretend I haven't heard. Nothing must happen to spoil our gay outing now!

"He had that cap pulled down over his head," persists the haro-san. "You know why? Because he didn't have any ears, that's why! It's a fact, that nice little guy didn't have any ears. How come, d'you suppose? He had scars on his neck as if he'd been burned deep—or as if some animal had clawed him. You suppose he's been mauled by an animal, Yuka-san?"

I nod vaguely. As he hasn't guessed the truth, let the matter rest there. Why tell him what sort of beast it was that ripped off the ears of the silkworm farmer and clawed my own arm to the bone? I know Sam-san well enough by now to realize that he's sensitve—too sensitive. Why should he suffer because of what happened in our city fourteen years ago?

"Ah, here we are!" I cry in perhaps evident relief. "The *buyens!* The lollipops!"

Sam-san inspects the plastic hair ornaments laid out on the counter. There are dozens of them, of all colors and sizes, but I know at once the ones I want—and those that want me. A moment later Sam-san is sticking the *buyens* with the dove-gray end-knobs into my hair. How lucky that he chose *them!* It's nice that we have the same taste.

"Holy smoke, Yuka-san!"

"What is it?"

"Why, it just dawned on me—how pretty you are!"

I know that I am blushing. Without waiting until Sam-san has paid for the *buyens,* I move on, and eventually find myself standing by the soda fountain, where couples, laughing and chatting, are eating their way through mountains of ice cream and gooey banana splits.

"What'll it be?" Sam-san asks, catching up with me.

I feel like a character in an American movie as we climb onto the high stools and give the soda clerk our order. How delightful it all is! My eyes meet Sam-san's, as the iced lemonade slowly mounts to our mouths through the transparent straws. We stop drinking to smile at each other, and I know, for certain now, that we have become friends.

Six

A bit of a slip-up! And it might have been avoided with a bit of cleverness on my part. I could have used some ruse to keep our lodger out a little later, thus preventing him from meeting our old painter friend, Maeda-san. But nowadays I live in a whirl. Busy making things nice for the haro-san, I'm on my feet from the moment I slide open the *fusuma* at dawn until I slip into my *futon* at night. That must be why I got my timetable mixed up.

Oh, sometimes I am so discouraged with myself!

Prudence and good sense are the basic virtues of Japanese womanhood, but I fail miserably in my efforts to be as nimble-witted as was my mama-san or as wise as my Aunt Matsui. Am I too frivolous by nature? Too fond of chatting, of singing, of playing the *samisen*? Dear me! This slip-up may cost us those future lodgers.

The moment I open our gate and see Maeda-san and my three neighbors sitting in a row on our bath-house bench, I remember that it's Wednesday evening, bath evening. Our bamboo gate is still warm from a long day's sunshine, but it feels chilly to my touch. Well, there's nothing for it but to bow low, to move forward smilingly, to repeat the required polite formulas for introducing people. Although I wink at our lodger, to tell him to come indoors with me, my efforts perish in the bud (to use a beautifully poetic Western expression) when Maeda-san turns on the foreigner one of his incomparable smiles.

"So pleased to meet my friend's honored guest!" Maeda-san can speak only in a hoarse whisper, but the look that accompanies his words makes one forget his damaged vocal chords. What is there about a delicate, fine person which instantly captivates? Maeda-san, a painter, looks upon himself as a garden, a small garden under intensive cultivation. Daily he clears a fresh patch within himself, digs it, weeds and waters it, and plants seeds in the new soil. In his gently persuasive way, he has hinted that I might well do the same. Otherwise, according to Maeda-san, one's inner being remains a wilderness, with poisonous snakes and rank weeds ready to choke everything.

Now, flicking the dust from our green bench, he invites our lodger to be seated, and Sam-san complies eagerly. Naturally! I mean, Sam-san is the sort of person who would be bound to realize *who* Maeda-san is, in spite of his hoarse, unlovely voice, in spite of his ruined skin. After another courteous bow, Maeda-san joins him on the bench while the three women kneel on the grass at a polite distance. Concealing my alarm beneath an especially bright smile, I turn toward the house.

"I beg you to excuse me. I must prepare my guest's supper," I cry.

However, I don't go to the kitchen. (I hadn't the slightest intention of going there.) A wise woman should never let a situation get out of hand, Aunt

Matsui has taught me. So I stand listening behind the *shojii,* prepared to rush out and snatch my lodger away, should Maeda-san's conversation become too frank—that is to say, too upsetting.

At first, however, everything seems to be going all right. Maeda-san keeps to the polite trivialities that are prescribed by good manners.

"Very pleased to hear you going to Miyajima Sunday. Am going also in company other friends. Hope meet you there, Mr. Willoughby."

(Quiet, Mrs. Bullfinch, *please!* Maeda-san's voice is so hoarse I can scarcely hear what he's saying. It taxes my hearing dreadfully to have to eavesdrop, with you singing so loudly, darling. You don't want me to wear out my eardrums, do you?)

"That'll be great, sir!" My lodger's voice is firm and enthusiastic (quite different from Maeda-san's strangled whisper), and he can't seem to take his eyes off my friend. In the lapel of his gray kimono the old painter wears his customary flower, and on his face is the gentle smile which is as much a part of it as his well-shaped chin and fine, straight nose.

"You enthusiast of *ofuro?*" he asks Sam-san, and I thank heaven he has chosen such a safe subject. When my lodger answers that he hasn't had the pleasure of taking a Japanese bath yet, Maeda-san asks if he'd like to be initiated into its ritual.

"I sure would! I want to know everything about this country," cries the haro-san, who has plenty of charm too, in his foreign way. Maeda-san, who's particular about people, likes him, I can see.

"Well, Japanese people absolutely crazy about hot water," Maeda-san explains. "You Americans crazy about cocktails, English crazy about tea, we Japanese—"

"Are known as the most bath-conscious people in the world," finishes Sam-san. "And the cleanest!"

"No doubt true," Maeda-san answers without false modesty. "Well then, my friend, most important thing to know about our *ofuro* is that water of bath not meant to wash in."

"Not to *wash* in?"

"No. Wash outside. Big tub only meant to warm self, rest and ease body. Now, my friend, bath cere-

[67]

mony goes like this. First, head of family hops into steaming bath, head of family hops out. Then son hops in, hops out. Mama-san hops in, hops out—"

"You mean the mother takes her bath *after* the son?" asks Sam-san, puzzled, and I feel myself blushing behind my *shojii*. What will my friends think of the American's uncouth question? Liking my young lodger so much, I want to dash out and defend him from their no doubt unkind thoughts.

"Naturally!" Maeda-san replies, and tactfully hurries on. "Now daughters climb into red-hot bath—and out. Then humble servant, if any. If household boasts small dog, dog takes his bath last."

"Well, that's one thing to be thankful for, anyhow!"

"Please?"

"Oh, nothing," says Sam-san, looking contrite.

Maeda-san holds up an elegant hand, stained with paint, like the hands of all painters, I suppose.

"One more thing!" he cries. "Before you take bath, my friend, remember always bow low to family, and say, '*Ho furoni*—am taking bath.' When come out, must bow again, proclaim, '*Ho furo mashita*—have had bath.' Understand?"

"*Ho furoni!*" cries our impetuous American, leaping to his feet. He looks happy, as if he is in the company of someone he really likes. "Say, where do I come in, in this bathing routine? *After* the dog?"

Maeda-san gives his charming and humorous smile. "Before everyone else, of course, for you are honored guest. Actually we are all waiting here for the water to heat. These three ladies come to take evening bath, like me." Maeda-san nods toward our neighbors, kneeling on the grass in their grease-stained *mompes*. (Oh, their poor old work pants really are a sight!)

"You see," he goes on, "lack of means prevents these ladies from owning own bath-house, so Yuka-san and myself invite to our houses twice each week. All very different from prewar days. Now we excluded from town's public baths, so—"

"*Excluded?*"

Ah, I knew it! The moment I dreaded has come at last.

"Tea is ready!" I cry gaily, hurrying out from behind my *shojii*. "Please come in, Sam-san."

I might have known it! Sam-san's streak of stubbornness, which I so admire, chooses this moment to turn into pig-headedness. He ignores me and my tea.

"*Why* excluded?" he persists obstinately.

"Because of our scars," answers Maeda-san softly. "Our keloid scars. You not realize you speaking to A-bomb victim, my friend?"

Now Maeda-san really has spilled the beans, as the Americans say. What's more, I think he did it on purpose. Tactful as he is, he would not have shocked a guest if he hadn't had a good reason.

"We here—Yuka-san and I and these ladies—just five out of hundred thousand survivors of A-bomb," Maeda-san goes on. "Many of us burned horribly, not to mention more serious damage inside. That reason why healthy Hiroshimans, most come here since war, wish avoid us. They say 'Ugh!' when see our keloid scars—rough, disgusting welts. Not wish look at naked bodies of A-bomb survivors in public baths."

For once I feel anger toward my dear old friend. Maeda-san, who knows the human heart from A to Z, ought to have sensed the inner vulnerability of this young American. Why, the most obvious thing about Sam-san is his sensitiveness! Why then does Maeda-san

not treat him with his usual delicacy? I must try to save
the situation.

"Shall I bring the tea out here?" I cry desperately.
No one answers me, but I hurry into the kitchen nevertheless, and rush back again with the tray.

The green tea looks pretty in my red lacquered
bowls, but although my *ofuro* visitors all bow charmingly as they accept my hospitality, they don't seem in
a mood to relax. I try to catch Maeda-san's eyes to warn
him. I even succeed and put my finger over my lips, but
to my surprise he shakes his head.

At that moment I understand that Maeda-san's way
is different from mine. Obviously he means to take
matters into his own hands. And suddenly I'm not angry with him any longer. I even feel a certain relief.

"Harada-san here typical A-bomb victim," the old
painter continues, and he exchanges a glance with one
of our three friends kneeling behind him on the grass.
"She asks me tell you not feel upset by her not-pretty
face. Too flat, she feels, as railway station luckily fell
on it. I say lucky, for cement protected Harada-san from
lethal radiation. Ah, my friend, Harada-san had terrible

experiences! Had nice flower-arrangement school—lost it. Had nice sons—lost them. Lost husband, lost health, lost beauty in one minute on famous August sixth. Now registered as day laborer at Municipal Office, like many impoverished survivors. Hacks up roads."

Sam-san has grown pale beneath his tan. He throws a quick look at Harada-san. Then his eyes don't seem to know where to fix themselves.

"Now Harada-san gets up in black dawn, walks miles on swollen legs," Maeda-san goes on, and I know that he means to tell Sam-san all. "After slaving long day, trudges to seashore to dig for edible clams, or to hills to hunt for herbs. Pay as laborer too little to buy enough rice to live. Also does *arubeit*. Sits up all night to get few *yen* more by working sideline job. Tears codfish to bits with fingers to make shredded codfish for restaurants. Very tough lonesome work, tearing fish in black night. Of course she only one in thousands—in ten thousands! Ah, my friend, is long time since Harada-san has laughed from bottom of heart."

Maeda-san stops speaking, and I glance quickly at the haro-san. And of course it's there, that look of dismay I dreaded, which I knew would come if he found out the truth about us and our street. But then my glance goes to Harada-san, and suddenly the foreigner doesn't seem to count any more. How strange! Yet ever since he came I've been making such giant efforts to deceive him.

I move softly across the young grass toward Harada-san. I kneel in front of her with my lacquered tray.

"Cha?" I say. *"Dozo?"*

Harada-san takes the round red tea bowl I hold out to her, and as our hands fleetingly touch, a spark of friendship passes between us. Ah, I wish I might press Harada-san in my arms as I once saw two Western women embrace each other in the railway station in Tokyo. But Japanese sorrow must ever remain inside. Our two pairs of eyes communicate nevertheless, and the steam rising from the hot tea mercifully veils Harada-san's unlovely features.

Something extraordinary happens then. Behind the cloud of steam I catch a glimpse of Harada-san as she was before the A-bomb ruined her features—young, lovely, and loved. Harada-san draws in her breath. She leans softly forward. In the pupils of my eyes she sees the true image of herself, and her poor face relaxes in a smile of gratitude. She gives a tinkling, a youthful laugh.

"*Arigato*," she whispers as she takes the tea. "Thank you!"

Over Harada-san's shoulder I can see Sam-san's face. How distressed his eyes look! Now he knows the truth. Will he flee from our misery and not recommend us to his friends?

Well, if he wishes to leave us, let him. Let him! For these are *my* people. My whole attention, my whole love, is turned on Harada-san. Gazing still at her own unblemished face mirrored in my eyes, she smiles. And I smile back at my friend through the steam that rises from the little red tea bowl.

Seven

If Sam-san were a Japanese he would pretend nothing had happened. Well, he isn't. His first glimpse beneath Hiroshima's outer shell has upset him badly, and he doesn't know how to hide it. The corners of his mouth are tense as he strolls up and down our garden after my other guests have left. The haro-san isn't himself at all.

I slip into the house, for it's clear that our lodger would like to be alone. In the kitchen I put rice in my earthenware pot and let water stream over it. Dear kitchen, how I love it! Small, bare, and lacking in every modern comfort, it's the place where I, like other Japanese women, feel most at home. Alone in my kitchen, I can give vent to my pent-up feelings and admit my worries, which I must suppress at all other times. Now I let my thoughts go to Fumio as I stand preparing the seaweed bouillon, and my fears, like black buzzards, swoop down on me.

Pong. Pong. I count the strikes and realize it's eight o'clock. Every evening it takes Fumio longer to walk from the garage to our house; every night he seems more tired when he arrives. (The Fumio I married could have run the whole distance in ten minutes, even in his outsize army boots.) I am so anxious that when I go to light the fire my fumbling fingers drop the match, burning a little hole in my *yukata*.

A burst of laughter shakes our house. Quickly I peer through the opening in the *shojii* and see that Sam-san and the children are settled on the floor, having a wonderful time. Sam-san is showing them how his big pocket handkerchief can suddenly become a rabbit with pointed ears. How easy, how natural the young American is—just as if he belonged to our family. Yet three days ago we'd never laid eyes on him. He's chosen to stay on here, sleeping on the floor and putting up with all sorts of discomforts, because he's happy in the atmosphere of our little home. With a lighter heart I return to my cooking. This will be the first dinner Sam-san has had with us.

There. At last I hear my husband's steps in the garden and the click of our bamboo gate opening and shutting. That's my signal to fill the wooden container with rice and pour the seaweed bouillon into our porcelain bowls with their pretty flower design. In the other room I can hear them saying hello to each other, and Michiko's *"Konichiwa, Papa-san."* I decide that this evening must be especially gay so that Sam-san won't think about those sad things he heard. Dear me, what a shame that Ohatsu's doing *arubeit!* Her pretty face (reminding him of Tosho Hamada's, perhaps?) always puts Sam-san into a happy mood.

"How snug you all look!" I cry as I draw open the *shojii* and see them gathered around the low dining table, beneath which the brazier burns warmly. Our big quilted cloth covers their knees, for although it's May, my husband has begun to feel chilly in the evening of late. That's why we still light the brazier at night.

Michiko is gravely teaching the haro-san how to use chopsticks.

"*Dozo*," my snowdrop says patiently. "Like this, Sammy."

"Michiko!" I cry, shocked.

"I told her to call me Sammy," explains my lodger, and he gives me that special smile of his. He puts his arm around Michiko and hugs her. "Don't scold Michiko, Yuka-san. She's my girl."

I put down the rice-container in the center of the table, and when I take off the lid a lovely cloud of steam sails upward. Sam-san maneuvers his ivory chopsticks comically.

"Who wants to bother with clumsy old knives and forks? I'm for chopsticks from now on!" he cries, and Fumio gives a grin. Oh, my dear husband, how happy I am when I see your pale lips turn upward! It's so rare nowadays. I send him a shy smile, then lower my eyes. It would embarrass Fumio if I showed my feelings for him in public, but a wave of affection sweeps between my husband and me.

I kneel beside Sam-san, placing a bowl of soup before him. The lid has a design of a yellow duck eating a pink frog.

"I hope that you'll enjoy our special seaweed bouillon, Sam-san. It's flavored with herbs that Ohatsu grew in the garden," I add slyly, to make him like it.

"Ohatsu grew them?"

Our lodger seems surprised that such a fragile creature as Ohatsu can actually tend a garden. Without so much as tasting his soup, he exclaims, "De-licious!" Then he casts a warm glance around our room. "Say, it sure is nice here!" he cries, and I can hear that he's the old Sam-san again.

I too look about the room and, seeing it with the foreigner's eyes, can appreciate it anew. It's so harmonious, so simple. Our wall-scroll, painted by Maeda-san, depicts a cluster of flowers, with the ancient Japanese text, "When once flowers bloom in your mind, the whole world will be filled with their fragrance." The actual flower arrangement beneath the scroll is so humble that it fills the spectator with humble thoughts, which is the true role of flowers, I think. (Three white tulips that ask for nothing, that wish only to give peace

to harassed hearts, rise out of a white vase.) Through
the sliding doors I make out the gleam of our old stone
lantern. It casts a benevolent light on our pale cherry
tree, whose buds still sleep in their swaddling clothes.

"This place is a *home!*" says the haro-san feelingly.
"You know, Yuka-san, it takes somebody like you to
make a house into a home, to make a man into a husband, to make children—well, look at those!"

I'm overcome with embarrassment. An old married
woman like me, over thirty, being showered with com-
pliments! Not knowing where to turn my eyes, I hide
my blushing face in Michiko's hair, and she throws her
arms around my neck. Life it *too* wonderful! To hide my
joy, I hurry into the kitchen, to return with de-
lectable raw fish, some pink, some white, together with
sliced pickled horseradishes. After sampling the festive
food, which I bought especially for the haro-san, I pour
out saké. Then I sit back, curling my toes in delight,
and watch my dear family eating and chatting.

Beneath the table five pairs of feet have grown
warm, and the heat spreads gently into our five pairs
of legs covered with the soft quilted cloth. Five pairs

of elbows are planted on the low table, while five happy faces savor the delicious odors of the food. Chopsticks are busy, saké cups are drained. As the rice wine trickles down our throats, our bellies too grow warm and gay. The heat from the brazier and the heat from the drink and food fills us with well-being.

My happiness is almost—unseemly. Realizing how much I love my family and my home, I feel suddenly ashamed. For years now I've thought only of rebuilding my own nest, of making it snug and comfortable, of bringing tidbits to my gaping young. Have I been too self-centered, too occupied with "me and mine"? There is so much to do in my martyred town; help is so urgently needed by the groups working for our shattered victims. Maeda-san tells me that I ought to give *them* my time and love. But does Maeda-san not ask too much of people?

"Hear, hear! Give me your attention, Yuka-san, Fumio-san!"

I bow expectantly to our guest, and Fumio too bows politely.

"I want to propose a toast to the two nicest people

I ever met," cries the haro-san. "A long life and a happy one to you both! A happy life to your children! And, since this is Japan, to all your honorable grandchildren too!" Sam-san laughs.

He's just a little bit tipsy, perhaps—but adorable. He drains his cup, then holds it out to me to be filled again.

"And now," cries Sam-san, "let's all drink—to happiness!"

I translate for Fumio, then pour out some drops of saké for the children. I lift my fragile cup, which has a red berry painted inside it. First I bow low to our guest, then I bow to my husband, then to my son, last to my daughter. Then I turn to my husband again and —oh! The warm saké spills over my hand. As I smiled at Fumio, our glances met, and what I saw in his dark young eyes was despair! They're ablaze with grief. Two teardrops well up, hover a moment on his long lashes, then run down his cheeks.

An icy hand grips my heart. I have to suppress a cry. Now I know that what happened to Fumio by the river was not a sunstroke. Fearful of losing control of myself, I spring to my feet, and as I back toward the *fu-suma* I murmur, "Please excuse me." I see the haro-san glance anxiously from me to Fumio, and realize that some deception is in order.

"My hand burned itself on the saké. Clumsy hand!" I cry, giving it a smack in punishment. Ah, good! I've made Sam-san smile, made my children laugh. While they give their own little paws noisy smacks, I slip out of the room.

In the kitchen, behind the *fusuma,* I thrust my face into the plastic shopping bag that hangs on the wall (my friend who taught me English sent it from Tokyo) and let the storm break. Silently I weep, beating my foot noiselessly against the floor, and I bite my lips so fiercely that I taste the blood. I mustn't make a sound, although I'm shaking with sobs. Fumio! Oh, Fumio!

Perhaps half a minute passes. Already in the back of my mind the thought is forming that I must hurry back. Our lodger will be wondering about me. My foot keeps kicking the floor, hurting itself, and I still sob convulsively. But *now!* I pull my face out of the smart

Tokyo bag and stifle my last sob. I smooth my hair and compose my face, forcing the corners of my lips upward. Up, up! I've prepared a bowl of bright green plums, which I snatch from the table. Holding it high before me, I walk back toward the others.

Eight

"Slugs! Oh, I'd love a world without slugs!"

Ohatsu kneels by her bed of flowers, picks one of the damp pests off a white pansy, and gazes worriedly into the flower's soiled face.

"I'd like to be rid of those dirty slugs for good!" small sister says passionately. Her voice is charged with feeling. Oh, I wish Ohatsu wouldn't put so much nervous emotion into everything she says and does! She likes her flowers too well. She worries about them too acutely. As she holds the slug between her forefinger and thumb, its damp brown horns wave back and forth in terror, and instantly Ohatsu transfers her feverish sympathy to it.

"Does it feel pain when it's—you know? Does it, do you think?"

She can't bear to pronounce the word "crushed," so sends me a meaningful look from the corners of her eyes. We're kneeling side by side, weeding, and so delicate is the green May night that Ohatsu, loath to shatter its tranquillity, speaks to me in a whisper. Her harassed concern for everything living is contagious. Suddenly I remember the cackling, the meowing, the frenzied barking with which Hiroshima's animal world suffered and died on the day of the holocaust. Yes, everything can suffer—even a slug, I suppose. I motion to her to let the wretched creature go free. As the slug, waving its crinkly horns, wriggles off gaily, Ohatsu and I exchange a smile.

It's nice to be alone with small sister, kneeling with her by her flower bed. It's nice to listen, together, to our crickets rustling their wings in the tree hole above our heads. Nice, too, to sniff the perfume of the acid weeds.

[86]

"Elder sister?"

"Yes?"

"I want to ask you something."

"What about?"

"About—love."

Dear me! I give a little laugh, but then throw a glance at Ohatsu and grow serious. Her breath is coming faster just because she has mentioned love—that magic word. Her bosom heaves. It's clear that Ohatsu is not only ready for the big event; she's avid for it. Alarmed, I ask her what she wants to know.

"Do you believe in love—at first sight, elder sister?"

Heavens, it *must* be the haro-san, incredible though it seems! To gain time, I pry a tough weed out of the ground, letting my thoughts pursue entirely new paths. An American husband for Ohatsu! We-l-l-l, as Sam-san would say, why not? Mightn't my thin sister put on a little weight in that prosperous country of his that has never known privations? Mightn't she sleep more calmly in the arms of a man to whom suffering is a stranger—sleep without waking up screaming? Oh, it would feel *safe* to have my frail plum-twig married to someone like Sam-san! Ohatsu may be smooth and unblemished on the outside, but her mind is rough with scars. Her heart has been battered out of shape from too early pain.

"*Do* you, elder sister?"

"Believe in love at first sight? Oh, of course!" I cry untruthfully, but then my conscience stabs me.

The fact is, I *don't* believe in love at first sight! Real love is the kind that grows slowly, like a tree, but the thought that small sister might have found a solution for her difficult life makes me sigh with contentment. Ohatsu is quick to read my mind.

"So then you *will* let me marry anyone I like? You won't let the *nakodo* marry me off?" she asks breathlessly as she slides her silken fingers into mine.

A caress is unusual from my shy Ohatsu, and I melt with tenderness at her touch. So disarmed am I that I don't put up any resistance at this suggestion that we do without the services of a matchmaker.

"Of course you may marry anyone you like, small sister."

Instantly she jumps to her feet. She presses her narrow hands to her breast—it is Ohatsu's most enchanting gesture—and passionately thanks me.

"Remember, you can't *un*promise now! You've given me your word," she cries, then giggles like the naïve little girl she is.

It is growing dark in our garden. Ohatsu's white pansies have turned lead-gray with the dusk, and at last we pick up our baskets and prepare to go into the house. Before sliding open the *shojii,* Ohatsu turns to look at the rows of pale pansies growing in her flower bed, and at the young white irises just showing their pointed faces. This year Ohatsu has planted only white flowers. The white irises will be followed by milk-white zinnias, the zinnias by snow-colored asters. And later on creamy chrysanthemums will bloom.

"White was her favorite color. I'm sure she'd like *white* bouquets this year," Ohatsu says to me, and from one moment to the next her voice has become strained.

"Stop it, darling!" I put my arm around small sister's suddenly tense body, as we move into the house. I am anxious about my sister; she lives too much in her childhood—a childhood she never had. Her experience on the day of the atom bomb has weighed her down; she is like a young pine on whose fragile branches too much snow fell at too early an age. Hiroshima is full of young people like Ohatsu, unharmed outwardly, inwardly crippled and twisted out of shape.

"Let's look at the things in our box, elder sister."

I knew it! She's in an upset mood now. Thinking of our mother has caused her to sink back into the past, and, as always at such moments, it is "our box" she wants. Our memory-box seems to be the one thing that soothes small sister's unhealed wounds.

Inside the house, Ohatsu speeds to fetch the box. Without turning on the lights, we kneel side by side before it on the *tatami*. Ohatsu, looking as excited as if she were seeing the lacquered box for the first time, plunges her hands into it.

"My—bell! Listen to it, elder sister!"

Ting-ting-ting.

To and fro in our dim room Ohatsu swings the silver bell which Mama-san's sister gave her for her third birthday. All the objects in "our box" were birthday gifts from Aunt Matsui, in whose house we used to keep the treasures she'd given us. (It was Aunt Matsui's idea, so that we needn't lug our toys back and forth on our weekly visits.) That certainly turned out to be a blessing. The toys we kept at our aunt's house in the suburbs remained beautifully intact, while everything in our own house was turned to ashes and whirled off into the sky.

"My glass goose!" Ohatsu cries. "And—look! My doll's chopsticks. How I love our box, elder sister!"

"So do I, darling."

My most cherished possession in "our box" is a rag doll. I take him out and arrange his crumpled kimono. The blue material of his *obi* is crushed, his *tabis* are all awry. Oh, how shabby Rag Doll is looking, how worn! I nestle him in the crook of my arm and rock him.

(Dearest Rag Doll, why do you look so worn and thin? Why do you look—so wasted? Do you know, Rag Doll, you're beginning to look a little bit like my Fumio. Or rather, Fumio's beginning to look like *you*. Lately, when he lies in bed, sleeping in the crook of my arm, so limp and exhausted . . . Oh, dear!)

"Rag doll looks awfully thin, don't you think, Ohatsu?"

"He was always thin, elder sister." Ohatsu smiles dreamily, ringing her silver bell in the soft twilight.

"Not as thin as he is now. He's getting to look—"

I stop in time. I must take hold of myself, not give

way to panicky fears. I mustn't let my frail sister see how worried I am about Fumio. Fortunately, before she has time to ask what I meant, there's an interruption. We hear steps outside, and our bamboo gate being softly opened and shut.

"*Dozo!* Are any of you dear people at home?"

There are voices which make one's skin tighten, one's defenses go up. The honeyed tones that reach my ears have had that effect on me ever since I was a child, but as old Nagai-san slithers into our room I receive her with extravagant politeness. She is a distant relative, in the first place, which calls for utmost courtesy on my part. In the second place she follows the profession of *nakodo*, which gives her additional prestige. Indeed, it was none other than Nagai-san who arranged my own marriage to Fumio. I utter a stream of polite speeches, telling our unwelcome visitor how welcome she is.

"Ah, it's months since we saw you, Nagai-san. Such a surprise! Ohatsu, will you bring Nagai-san some tea, please? Meanwhile, I'll turn on the lights. There! Now tell me, how has your honored health been, Nagai-san? What lucky star brought you to see us this evening?"

But I needn't have asked. As Ohatsu moves toward the kitchen, the old matchmaker's glance crawls up my sister's body and settles on the nape of her lovely neck.

"A beauty! A *great* beauty, in fact," she whispers, kneeling beside me on the floor and talking from behind her snuff-colored silk fan. (How well I remember that fan from the days she used to call here, when she was arranging my marriage with Fumio.) "No wonder that the young men, that *one* young man in particular—"

"I'm afraid you are wrong, Nagai-san. There is no young man."

"Much you know! The family's always the last to hear of it, my dear. There *is* a young man, let me assure you, and what with these modern 'love marriages' all the rage, you are going to wake up one fine day and find your little bird flown."

I giggle respectfully, implying that Nagai-san has meant this only as a joke. But then I remember Ohatsu's asking that very evening for my permission to marry anyone she chose. Dear me! Has the old witch really ferreted out something? Beware of women with long noses, my Aunt Matsui always warns me, and Nagai-san, like every matchmaker, has an extraordinarily long nose. The tip of it is always wiggling, as though she were sniffing a scent.

Now she has slid closer to me on her knees. She is still whispering behind her fan.

"To tell you the truth, my dear, I dropped in today to talk to you about Ohatsu. We mustn't lose a minute in marrying her off—to the *right* man, of course. Now there's a certain gentleman I know, a very distinguished gentleman—"

"How is your rheumatism, Nagai-san?" I break in.

"You mean my lumbago." Nagai-san looks offended. "It's much worse. Well, now, I've said a few words to this distinguished gentleman about Ohatsu, and—"

"So very kind of you to have troubled about us, Nagai-san! What with your lumbago and all, you really mustn't work so hard. You should take it a little easy. Please don't trouble about small sister."

(Trouble! As if she wasn't counting on financial "thanks" from the "distinguished gentleman"!) Her greedy eyes snap, yet her voice is honeyed as she assures me that she's only doing her duty.

"I married you off, didn't I, my dear? And at the age

of sixteen. Now I'll arrange for your young sister too. But we mustn't waste any time. This distinguished gentleman is in a great hurry. He-he! You see, he is— er—not in his first youth, to say the least, and he really *can't* wait very long—"

Crash!

A cup has shattered on the floor in the kitchen, and we both know it was thrown, not dropped. Oh, this will never do! It may mean disaster if we get the *nakodo* against us. The poison she'd exude would penetrate every nook and cranny. It could ruin us.

"Please excuse me a moment, honored Nagai-san!" I cry distractedly.

I speed into the kitchen—but no trace of Ohatsu. It isn't the first time she's run away when her outraged feelings have become too much for her, and each time she does it I quake with fear. Is she racing through our darkened streets, her slender hands pressed to her breast? Is she kneeling by the river at the spot where our mama-san . . . Is she longing to follow . . . ?

"Yuka!" comes the matchmaker's voice. "I've only got a moment, dear girl. What's keeping you?"

"I am coming, Nagai-san."

Quickly I prepare a tray with refreshments and take it into the other room. I assume an expression of concern, bow apologetically.

"Ohatsu's been called away. Our neighbor's little daughter just—just fell into the well." (What a stupid lie.) "May I serve you some green tea, Nagai-san? Shall I run out and buy you some *suchi* from the fish shop across the street?"

"A little tea, if you please. No *suchi*. I just looked in on the off chance of finding you at home. But don't worry, I'll be back. Ah, dear girl, we go-betweens must have endless perseverance. Patience is, so to speak, our stock in trade."

"A cake?" I murmur. "*Dozo*, Nagai-san."

After that, for what seems an eternity, we kneel opposite each other on the *tatami*, sipping our tea and exchanging polite chatter about the family, about acquaintances. An hour, the rigidly prescribed period for a visit, crawls by. When at last we have finished our refreshments, we bow so low that our heads knock together like two hard-boiled eggs. Swiftly we get to our feet, and, as the old *nakodo* shuffles, pigeon-toed, to-

ward the *shojii,* she is fanning her sore head with her
snuff-colored fan.

"Speaking of elderly gentlemen being in a hurry to
get married, there may be some urgency on the part of
beautiful Ohatsu as well," she prattles on. "Yes, yes,
dear girl, we had better look facts in the face. Your
young sister is desirable today—but tomorrow? What's
more, there's the question of children, as you must realize. What sort of children will dear Ohatsu bear? Eh?
There's so much talk in Hiroshima nowadays about
you atom-bomb survivors having—er—strange children. Ah, it's all very sad, dear girl. But what I mean is
that we'd better hurry. In fact there's not a minute to
lose! You know as well as I that no family welcomes an
atom-bomb survivor as a daughter-in-law. However,
this distinguished old gentleman . . ."

"*Sayonara! Arigato. Gozai mashita.*"

"*Sayonara! Yoku irashite kudasai mashita.*"

We smile at each other falsely; we bow profoundly,
this time taking good care not to bump our heads.
When at long last we straighten up, the matchmaker
sends me a swift glance. Then her sharp little tongue

passes over her lips. She knows that she's scored a victory! In my eyes she has read the nameless fear that lurks in every Hiroshima survivor. For weren't both Ohatsu and I exposed to radioactive rays that penetrated our bones fourteen years ago? We are children of the bomb, and our own children are children of the bomb as well, for its mark may pass from generation to generation. Will it be the fate of my Michiko, of my fat Tadeo, of beautiful Ohatsu, to give birth to . . . to . . .

"*Arigato. Gozai mashita,* honored Nagai-san," I murmur tremblingly.

But the old *nakodo* is already scurrying off through my dark garden, carrying away all the peace of my heart.

Nine

After a long winter, what a treat to sit beneath a flowering cherry tree! The blossoms burst forth in the hot sun; the grass pushes itself out of the ground like green, eager fingers. (My son Tadeo tears up some blades and *eats* them.) The sky trembles with heat. Like most of the holiday-makers, we've brought our own straw mat, and we kneel on it in a circle, myself in the center. I strum my dear *samisen.*

"La . . . la-la . . . la . . ."

I love to play, and to sing. I've made up scores of

songs, rather the way insects make up theirs, I imagine. A scrap of melody, a few words explaining the fall of a petal, because its hour has come—things like that.

"Small sister, why aren't you singing? *Dozo*, sing," I cry.

"All light, elder sister," Ohatsu answers in English. But she sings in an absent-minded way, as though her thoughts were far off. What's wrong with my little sister? I ask myself. Suddenly she breaks off her cherry-blossom song so abruptly that I wince.

"Don't forget that we're meeting Maeda-san at the tea house," she whispers to me. "It's almost four now, elder sister."

Heavens, think of Ohatsu knowing the time! Something *must* be going on. And why does that baffling child ignore Sam-san's efforts to chat with her?

"Who wants saké?" I cry, a little rattled.

"I'd say everyone." The haro-san laughs. "We're having ourselves a ball."

If his country would parachute down a few thousand young men like Sam-san—so easy-going, so appreciative—we'd all love Americans. How he enjoys our modest party! Entering into our Japanese holiday mood (we treat our rare outings as if they were candies, sucking them slowly until nothing is left), our lodger downs saké, sings merrily, and makes jokes as gay and silly as our own. He was even enthusiastic about our choppy ride to Miyajima Island, although the ferryboat was so overloaded that it almost sank.

Now he looks about him at the groups of holiday-makers kneeling on their straw mats. Businessmen have brought their pale-faced clerks out for a saké spree, and many factory-owners are treating their workers to raw fish beneath the cherry trees. Happy to be rid of their responsibilities for one day, young men are hopping about tipsily, and the "baby-sans," as my lodger calls Tadeo and Michiko, jump to their feet and perform a ballet of their own in the new kimonos that Maeda-san has given them. These spring kimonos are patterned with miniature Mount Fujis, whose craters smoke cheerfully. Everyone applauds them.

"Now *you* sing a song, Yuka," my husband begs.

He looks well in the sunshine, and I am reassured, certain the warm spring winds will blow health back into him. I send him a smile and compose a *tanka* in his honor, saying that, with the arrival of the swallows and the cherry blossoms, our fortunes too will bloom. "La . . . la-la . . . la . . ." I sing.

When I've finished, we remain silent, overcome with well-being. Even my cheery Sam-san is silent and still. His gaze lingers on Ohatsu, whose loveliness matches that of the young May day. But suddenly our beauty leaps to her feet.

"Four o'clock, elder sister!" Urgency puts a harsh sound into her silken voice. "Almost five minutes past four."

The impetuous child hooks her thin fingers in mine, jerking me up. She laughs exultantly, like an excited small girl, as she pulls me across the grass. Ohatsu's expression is so radiant that people stop and smile after her. But, as always, small sister is oblivious to admiration.

"There! There he is," she cries.

"Maeda-san?"

"No, no. My friend! My friend whom I told you about yesterday."

We have stopped. The shouting, laughing holiday crowds before the tea houses—venerable grandparents, students, children clinging to their parents' hands—

move like a surging sea around Ohatsu and myself. She is looking in the direction of the Red Dragon Tea House, where we're to meet our host, Maeda-san.

"That's the one—Hiroo! On the steps, in the dark green kimono."

She pushes her trembling fingers into my hand and in a rush of words confides to me that she has fallen in love "for all eternity," like the legendary Ohatsu. It is strange, but the object of her affection bears a striking resemblance to the classical Ohatsu's lover as he's depicted in old Japanese prints.

"He *is* handsome, isn't he, elder sister?" Ohatsu asks me, and watches my eyes widen with admiration.

Handsome? He's a young *god!* "Yes," I whisper breathlessly. (Oh, I shouldn't, of course! I know nothing whatsoever about this beautiful youth and have no right to encourage Ohatsu. But, dear me, I do love a romance!)

Ohatsu tells me that her young man is a painter, a pupil of Maeda-san, through whom she met him. As paintings are difficult to sell, he is being forced to earn his living as a newspaper photographer.

[103]

"Well, what of it?" I ask, trying to make my voice impersonal.

"He wants to *marry* me!"

Ohatsu gazes ecstatically toward the tea-house steps. We are standing beneath a cherry tree, and a flurry of blossoms drifts down onto her eloquently clasped hands. My heart is wrung. Small sister! She looks as frail as those white flowers, whose life on earth is already over. Yet Ohatsu has survived the greatest massacre that mankind has ever known. Her petal-like body was preserved from the conflagration on the bank of the Hiroshima river, into which our mother leaped to her death.

"Ohatsu . . ." I begin, and my voice, which should have been stern, shakes with affection.

"Elder sister, you promised! You can't go back on your word now. You said I might marry anyone I choose."

What to say? How to act? While I'm considering this, I note that the handsome youth has caught sight of us and is flying toward small sister on "the wings of love." (How delicately Westerners express themselves, in spite of their unpoetic looks.) Dear me! Before I've decided what manner to adopt, Ohatsu has introduced us, and Hiroo Shimizu and I bow and smile, bow and smile again. At this critical moment my family appears beside us.

"Ah, there you are!" I cry, pretending composure, for Aunt Matsui says that countenance is all-important —act flustered, and you've lost the game. Yet I am blushing as furiously as small sister as I present Ohatsu's admirer to Sam-san and to my husband.

"Shimizu-san is a good friend of Ohatsu's," I say, and our lodger's face falls.

Mine changes expression too, for I realize that my dreams for small sister have collapsed like a bamboo shack in a typhoon. From the look in the haro-san's eyes I know that the sudden appearance of Ohatsu's young man is a most unpleasant surprise for him. It must be obvious to him, as to everyone, that Ohatsu is hopelessly in love with the godlike Hiroo. Dear me! In a second it is clear to me that Sam-san never *did* have a chance with small sister.

"We're all waiting for you, dearest friends!" Down, down the long tea-house steps hurry Maeda-san's merry-sounding *getas*.

"We'll spend a festive evening together amidst splendid cherry blossoms," he cries, and his eyes are so loving that even his hoarse, ruined voice warms one. In a second he has cleverly taken in the situation (Ohatsu and Hiroo obviously enamored of each other, the haro-san about to turn grouchy). Instantly Maeda-san snatches a spray of cherry blossom from his *obi* and presents it to Sam-san.

"Overjoyed you could join our cherry-blossom *furi!*" he says with his wonderful smile, and fastens the flowering twig in Sam-san's buttonhole. "Party will be doubly nice because having you with us, dear friend. Happy hours lie ahead."

Yes, happy, happy hours! How lucky I am. Here I sit in a tasteful tea house, listening to *samisen* music and eating food so prettily prepared that I shall have to draw little pictures of the various dishes in order to explain them to Harada-san and the other unfortunate people in my street. Fish eyes, for example, sleeping on beds of fragrant seaweed. And bees dipped in batter, fried to a crisp and mounted on elegant toothpicks. Heavens, how different party food is from our monotonous daily fare, how much more different still from the hateful rice gruel which is all that Harada-san can afford to eat.

"*Banzai! Banzai!*"

"*Banzai,* Sam-san!" I cry. Our little party is getting tipsy because of all these toasts, and Sam-san is crimson in the face. Still he's not in a good humor and keeps filling his glass and throwing glances at Ohatsu and Hiroo, who are kneeling side by side at one end of the long, low table. "Have something nice—have a fish eye," I implore him.

"Thanks. I'm not hungry."

It's clear that Sam-san is envious—not of Hiroo for having captured Ohatsu, but of the two of them for having found happiness together. But now what's up? Ear-splitting applause reaches us from way down the table.

"Ah, the games have begun. How lovely!" I cry, seeing that a baseball game is on at the other end of the long room. Of course there isn't a real ball, and the bats aren't real either, but the guests are going through the motions of baseball, swinging their arms as they pretend to bat, then catching an imaginary ball that comes flying through the air. It's really a sort of ballet.

I jump to my feet and hurry off to join the game with Maeda-san and his artist friends. What fun they're all having! Two geishas, hired for the occasion, have joined us, and while they play their *samisens* the rest of us sing, imitating the gestures of baseball players.

After that we begin to play "train," which is my favorite game. With our hands on one another's shoulders, we race up and down the long room, whispering, "Choo-choo! Choo-choo!"

I dash back, almost tripping over my long kimono, to refill Sam-san's saké cup and beg him to join the fun. "Come and play 'choo-choo' with me, Sam-san!"

"You're a *child*, Yuka-san. All you Japanese are just —children," the American says, but I only laugh and drag him to the far end of the room, where another game is about to start.

I explain to him that this one is called "The old hag, the hunter, and the bear" and that it's played in all the tea houses of Japan. It's a two-person game, I tell him, in which each player, hidden from the other by a tall screen, pretends to be either a wicked old woman (hobbling along with bent back) or a hunter (stalking his prey) or a bear (advancing on all fours).

"The audience can see *both* players, so it knows from the start who's going to win. But it's not till they reach the end of the screen that the players can see each other. Do you—dig it?" I ask Sam-san, laughing teasingly.

"I must be dumb."

"But it's not complicated at all! The old hag can scold the hunter, but she gets eaten up by the bear. The hunter can kill the bear, but he's lost if he meets the old woman. It's great fun, Sam-san. We'll all laugh ourselves sick."

"You *will?*"

The haro-san doesn't sound convinced, but I tell him that Fumio and I will demonstrate for him. We jump to our feet, smile at each other, then take up our positions on opposite sides of the tall screen. Whom shall I act out? I ask myself when I'm alone, and decide to take the part of the hunter. So I advance toward the end of the screen with an imaginary knife held before me, to find Fumio awaiting me there, transformed into a harridan. The old hag scolds me roundly, to the delight of our audience. He's a wonderful actor, my Fumio. How he loves fun, loves life!

For round two I decide that *I* will act the old woman, and I hobble the length of the screen with the aid of a non-existent stick. Again Fumio has beaten me! There he is on all fours, shaking his bear head at me and growling, about to gobble me up. Everyone screams with laughter as the frightening bear topples over comically and lies on his side—everyone, that is, except me, for I can see the look on Fumio's face, and I realize that he's not play-acting any more.

I drop down on my knees beside him, and my poor husband gazes up at me with terrified eyes. The sweat is pouring down his face.

"I can't—get up," he whispers weakly.

As I open my mouth to call out, Fumio puts a restraining hand on mine. "Don't—tell anyone what's happened. It would spoil their evening. Yuka—it's come! *The illness* has come . . ."

Fumio's voice fades, and I see that he has fainted. Once more I open my mouth to call out, but I manage to hold back the scream that is rising in my throat. My husband is right (Fumio is always right). It would be inconsiderate to spoil our fellow guests' evening; they have little enough fun in their lives. Kneeling by my husband's prostrate body, I bow deeply to our friends.

"Please forgive us," I say, and smile at them. "A little accident, but nothing serious. Please forgive us. *Dozo.*"

Ten

Expensive apple, I'm annoyed with you. Every item in
this hospital shop costs too much, even the cheap little
celluloid comb I've just priced. I keep asking the saleslady, "How much?" (as I indicate a bag of caramels, a
paper fan, a game of *go*) and I realize that *"Ikura de-
suka?"* will be my usual question from now on. I've always been poor, but with Fumio ill I shall be destitute
—a thought that makes me feel a little faint. I dislike
people who demand much of life, but to be like Ha-

rada-san, not able to buy even an apple, will take getting used to.

"Maliryn Monloe," says the gray-faced saleslady. "That's her picture on the fan, next to Mount Fuji. It's torn; you can have it for half-price."

She looks as if an evil-smelling herring were dangling beneath her nose, no doubt because the odor of disinfectants and medicine is with her from morning to night. A hospital has a perfume of its own, there's no denying it, and I advise myself instantly to accept that smell. It's going to be part of my existence from now on. Isn't it better manners to come to terms quickly with what life offers one? It's more gracious.

"I'm not really intending to buy anything. I was just looking," I tell the saleslady untruthfully. "My husband . . ."

But at the very thought of Fumio, lying suffering upstairs, the corridor begins to sway. As I take hold of the counter, I hear the saleslady ask which is my husband's ward. When I answer that he's in the section for radiation sickness, her manner miraculously changes. She simply thrusts her expensive apple at me.

"Take it! It's yours." Her scarred cheeks quiver. "My family got burned up by the atom bomb. Excuse me for mentioning it," she humbly adds.

We bow to each other. She has contolled the twitching of her face, which is masklike again now, but our eyes meet in a long look. As another customer hobbles up, she whispers to me to wait, for she wants to wrap Fumio's apple in gift paper. (Oh, it feels as if she'd reached out her fingers and stroked my heart.)

"Thank you," I whisper back.

I lean against the wall and think of Fumio. In the ward upstairs my husband is battling against extinction —that is, his blood, liver, and spleen are battling, while Fumio lies gazing at a gay squirrel that perches on his window sill. He and his five roommates were all staring wistfully at the squirrel when I left them a moment ago. It's understandable. I mean, death sneaked into the bodies of those young men thirteen years back, and now it is finishing them off, while that gay squirrel . . .

I close my eyes (the saleslady is still busy) and let my tired body sag against the hospital wall. I didn't sleep the whole of last night—I spent it kneeling be-side Fumio's bed—but that isn't the main reason for my exhaustion. I'm worn out because I've been think-ing thoughts that are too big for me.

For instance, I keep thinking of the part that pure chance plays in our lives. If Fumio hadn't been given a furlough from the army on that famous August 6, 1945, he wouldn't have found himself in Hiroshima. And if he hadn't been in Hiroshima, he couldn't have gone searching for me through those piles of dead bod-ies, lifting corpse after corpse in an effort to find me, and so would never have come down with radiation sickness. He'd be well now, and able to plan a happy future for the four of us. As it is, his liver is doing all the planning, and what it plans is to die and take Fumio with it. Now that's what I call "too big thoughts."

"Asleep on your feet, Yuka-san?"

"Sam-san!"

Long-legged, tousle-haired, anxious-eyed, the Ameri-can has borne down on me. Quickly I try to rearrange my worried face.

"You've come to visit Fumio?" I ask. "He's sleep-ing. I'm sorry, Sam-san, but no one can see him."

"Good Lord, Yuka-san, why didn't you tell me Fumio was *that* sick?"

The haro-san seems terribly upset. Only now does he understand what happened to Fumio last night, and, as usual, he doesn't know how to hide his feelings. His distress breaks down my own composure and brings the tears to my eyes. I'm struggling to regain control of myself when I feel an object being slipped into my hand, and I realize that my new friend, the saleslady, has come to my rescue. As I close my fingers around Fumio's gift-wrapped apple I gaze at her disciplined features as a young actress might gaze at a great star from whom she wishes to take a lesson. The two of us smile brightly at each other. We bow many times.

"Now Sam-san, why don't you go home and wait for me there? Fumio can't have visitors," I tell the American and am happy to hear that my voice is normal.

What I've said isn't true, but the fact is I don't want Sam-san to see Fumio—or his roommates either. The time is past when I could hide things from him, but I like my young lodger too well to expose him to unnecessary horror. Sam-san's a free man still, but once pity enters him (and with pity the urge to help), he may remain free no longer. I want him to stay *outside* the tragedy of Hiroshima.

If only Dr. Domoto hadn't wandered along just then, everything would have turned out all right. But the nice cheery doctor rushes by, then stops and grasps my arm, his clever eyes sparkling at me from behind his thick glasses.

"Ha! Am just on way to husband, Mrs. Nakamura," he cries in his English, which is not too good.

I introduce Sam-san to him, and then the one thing happens that I *don't* want. Dr. Domoto, who's very proud of the hospital's new wing for radiation patients, invites Sam-san to come upstairs with us. So fate has taken matters out of my hands, and silently I mount the stairs, luckily remembering my manners and keeping three steps behind the gentlemen. As Dr. Domoto opens the door of Fumio's room, however, Sam-san turns and gives me a reproachful look. How could you keep all this secret from me? his eyes seem to ask. From *me*, Yuka-san!

"Squirrel's building his nest in the tree hole outside my window," Fumio whispers to me when the doctor

[118]

has greeted him and passed on to the next bed.
"*Is* he, my darling?"

Hands that I know intimately, that I respect and
honor, lie swollen on my husband's bed quilt. Even in
this short time they have become monstrous strangers,
and because the haro-san is standing beside me I
quickly cover them with my own hand. I nod toward
the bushy tail quivering with life, that protrudes from a
hole in the flowering cherry tree outside.

"Do you suppose his wife is sitting on eggs in there,
Fumio?"

I've made my suffering husband smile!

"Of course she is. Lots of eggs." His voice is a hoarse
whisper, and his features are drawn from the pain in
his distended belly. Still, my heroic Fumio can find
pleasure in that sight outside his hospital window. My
silly joke about "eggs" is repeated from bed to bed, and
in the disfigured faces smiles are born. The boy whose
hand has been twisted for fourteen years, so that the
fingers look like brown shriveled tree-roots, cries excitedly, "We've decided there must be young ones in the
nest. Yes, we're almost certain," he tells me, and the

five scarred heads on the hospital pillows staunchly nod. We're almost certain, the wistful eyes seem to say.

"Man in this bed has had twentieth operation," Dr. Domoto is explaining to Sam-san. "This fellow, young keloid victim; one-third of body covered with keloid scars. Ugh—English! I can't speak her," cries the doctor, and he tosses me a handful of Japanese words to interpret. With my hand on Fumio's suffering fingers, with my eyes fixed on the joyous cherry tree, I slowly translate.

"The doctor says that atom-bomb patients suffer from both external and internal injuries. Countless operations can sometimes remove keloid scars and other marks of the bomb. For the internal damage there's no remedy."

Sam-san nods. He is staring at the hideous welts that are visible on the patient's chest and shoulders, and the concentrated look on his face reminds me of the fact that his own father was a doctor. Perhaps Sam-san should have been a doctor too, as he told me that first evening he had hoped to be. Perhaps he still will be one, some day.

"Boy in this bed—contraction of eyelids due atom blast." Dr. Domoto takes over again, speaking in English. "Fourteen years sleeps with eyes open—or *doesn't* sleep. Both earlobes gone. Mouth—well, can see yourself what's happened to mouth. . . ."

He explains each case scientifically, sometimes turning down the bed sheets to show the visitor some new horror. As I listen to the doctor's voice, I wonder what the "cases" themselves think. Luckily they don't understand English. Even if they did, they probably would not be especially interested in hearing why most of them are doomed to die. Their eyes, glued to the squirrel's red tail, seem to be seeking the answer to a greater mystery—the mystery of life. Are they asking themselves why man, who couldn't create a single hair of that squirrel's tail, has made himself an expert in the destruction of living beings?

A hand lays itself on top of mine, presses it briefly. For a moment our three hands—the doctor's, my husband's, and mine—cling together in understanding. Then they move softly apart. And while the doctor quietly converses with Fumio, I turn my head and meet Sam-san's gaze.

But what has happened to the haro-san? The look in his eyes has changed. Perhaps it is because he's no longer a person watching from the outside; he's on the *inside* now. Since he stepped into Fumio's room, he has begun to take part in our tragedy, our life. Oh, of course Sam-san knew the facts of Hiroshima, but knowing facts is one thing, and it's another to stand in a room with six suffering men—not just watching them—suffering too. And wanting to help.

"Is there—is there anything I can do for Fumio?" he asks in a tense voice.

His tone is so anxious, so grave, that for a second my husband leaves off gazing at the bushy tail of the squirrel and smiles at our lodger.

"Ask him to buy the squirrel some nuts," says Fumio when I've translated the question, but at this Sam-san looks startled, almost as if he'd been given a slap in the face.

"Nuts? Just—nuts? Is *that* all I can do?"

Sam-san backs toward the door slowly. Before opening it, he lets his gaze circle the room, going from one to the other of the six beds with their loads of pain.

Then such a violent blush floods his face that one would think the rest of his body had been drained of all blood.

Our lodger makes a desperate little bow. He turns and hurries from the room.

Eleven

I like the dawn. One's day belongs to many people, but dawn belongs only to oneself. Like me, my daughter Michiko loves those early secret hours, perhaps because she was conceived at dawn, born at dawn. Every morning before the pink glow my little girl slips into the garden, and I know how she hopes, *hopes* that no one will follow her. At her age I did the same. Like Michiko, I had a date with my secret self. Tiptoeing to those trysts, I felt my breath come fast, as later on when I hurried to a lovers' meeting.

"Mama . . ." I hear her whisper every morning, and I hasten to give a reassuring little snore. (Did my mother also feign sleep when I breathed her name before running off to my dawn trysts? Mama-san, delicate Mama-san, I am sure you did.)

As I hear the *shojii* slide back, I open my eyes and see a little barefoot figure in a blue *yukata* tiptoeing out. I lie as still as a wax doll beneath my covers. Instinctively, then, I reach out my hand for Fumio, and when I remember that he isn't there I come fully awake. I slip out of my night kimono, pull on my *yukata,* and cross the floor silently so as not to awaken my fat baby boy. (I can hear him laugh in his sleep.) In the kitchen I hurry to light the fire. A bowl of steaming tea will heat my lonely body, which no longer has a mate to keep it warm.

Dear me, I have awakened Mrs. Bullfinch. I hear her stretching her matchlike legs and ruffling her feathers, although her cage is still covered with a cloth. When I lift a corner of it, she instantly opens her yellow beak. No, no, Mrs. Bullfinch, I beg. Don't twitter yet; you'll wake up my Tadeo. Oh, what a sour look Mrs. Bullfinch sends me! Very well, then, I give in.

You may chirp, Mrs. Bullfinch—but in a whisper, darling, chirp in a whisper.

Psch!

That's the tea water come to a boil. My noisy old kettle whistles away, and as I hurry to lift it off the fire it seems to throw me as grumpy a look as Mrs. Bullfinch's. Of course it likes to whistle, that's understandable. Whistling is our kettle's only mode of expression, as Fumio used to say. Instantly I catch myself up. Used to! Why *used* to? Oh, Fumio!

I brew myself a bowl of tea and, as I sip it, wander over to the sliding door. Putting my eye to the crack, I see Michiko crouching by our pond. Silent and motionless, she kneels on the grass, and her eyes are fastened on the lotus buds sleeping on the water. I feel my breath come fast. Ah, you too, Michiko? Do you too thrill at seeing things unfold, at watching beginnings? How much alike we are!

Kneeling there in the stillness of dawn, my daughter looks tensely expectant. She leans her head sideways, listening for the sound of the lotus buds unfurling. Poignantly I recall how some burst open with a little pop, others with a sound like a kiss. I see my daughter smile. A look of deep contentment lights up her round face, and I realize that Michiko has just witnessed a miracle—the birth of a brand-new flower on a brand-new spring morning. I too smile secretly behind the sheltering *shojii*.

"Catch, Michiko!"

I see a green ball whizzing through the air before I see the hand that threw it or the body to which the hand belongs. But my young lodger has grown so familiar to me that I can visualize his long bare legs in the too short *yukata* I've lent him, long before he comes ambling from our house.

"Are you watching for frogs, Michiko?" Sam-san asks her.

Michiko frowns. She puzzles over the English words, then shakes her head softly. She keeps shaking her round head, and I realize that she will never tell anyone what she has just seen. Until the end of her days she will keep her knowledge locked up behind that strangely secret smile.

Now she has sprung to her feet and is bowing low in her blue *yukata*. Her eyes are solemn in performing that act of courtesy—and she looks enchanting. Suddenly there comes over me that strange feeling of guilt which I have now and then at the thought that I love my family too much. But why should I feel ashamed of an emotion so natural to any woman? How am I guilty?

As if in answer, three ghostlike figures flit by our gate—Harada-san and her two friends trudging off to their day's work. (They are breaking stones for a new road some miles outside the city.) Ah yes, my feelings of guilt are certainly understandable. I've been neglecting my old friends, giving all my time to my own family, forgetting that the first duty of us bomb survivors is toward each other. I used to go out among them, helping. Now, like a moss-covered stone, I've become coated with selfishness. . . .

"*Konichiwa,* Harada-san!"

Michiko, beside the pond, is bowing to our three neighbors, who gravely return the bow. Then they catch sight of the haro-san and bow to him too—three tired women in grimy work pants, into which they have tucked their unwieldy kimonos. The young foreigner bows back, and I have the feeling that he could not have performed that Japanese salutation with sincerity a week ago. There's no doubt about it; something has happened to the haro-san in these days since he came to Hiroshima.

I press closer to the crack in the *shojii* and see Sam-san gazing after my friends. He's frowning. Suddenly he bends down and reaches out his arms to Michiko. My daughter runs into his embrace, and as Sam-san presses her to him I sense in him a desire to protect the child from the fate that has befallen Harada-san and those others, that has stricken all of us here in Hiroshima. His grave expression surprises me. And yet did I not guess from the very first that behind this young American's boyish ways, beneath his joking, lay another Sam-san, pining to unfurl—like the buds of the lotus flower?

As I watch, his fair hair is lit up by the sun, and all the slanting roofs in our street and the branches of our one cherry tree burst into flame. The sun, the sun! I slide open the *shojii* and am about to run out into the morning, when a thought freezes me. The tree outside my husband's window at the hospital must be all lit up too. The morning will be coming to him as it is coming to me. But for him and for those five other men the new day will not bring exultation. It is only one day closer to death. I fight down a shudder, and for a second lean my head against the *shojii*. To wake up on a sun-bathed morning like this and whirl about the garden with Michiko while her father watched us smilingly was one of those joys which ended the day before yesterday. Yes, only the day before yesterday.

Wham!

The green ball again. It whizzes straight at me, forcing me to act, not think. I grab it and throw it to Michiko, who tosses it to Sam-san, and within seconds a game is in full swing. How gay! For the moment I forget everything in the zest of the sport, for I've always been good at ball games.

"Yuka-san, for a girl you're not too bad. Bad—but not *too* bad!" Sam-san chuckles.

When I said good-by to him at the hospital yesterday, I was afraid our next meeting would be painful, but this young American is full of tact and delicate understanding. He knows that this is not the time to mention my tragedy, even though, in a way, we share in it now. I smile back at him. He makes me feel wonderfully relaxed.

Michiko stops playing, hurries up to me on her bare, dusty feet.

"Mama-san, Yamaguchi-san is coming down the street!"

I drop the ball. As I hear it go hopping along the garden path, it seems to me that gaiety itself is bouncing away from me.

"What is it, Yuka-san?"

I shush our lodger, finger on my lips, hoping against hope that if Yamaguchi-san doesn't hear us he will go away. As if a landlord could be discouraged, once he has smelled blood! Without a doubt Yamaguchi-san has heard the bad news already, and I know that he's all too anxious to evict us. For a long time he's had it in mind to build a row of modern, shiny houses which will bring him in many times his present rentals.

"Ah, good morning, good morning, Nakamura-san!"

So the leech is after us, just as I thought! It's with a great effort that I force myself to bow to the little man in the natty suit and the jaunty Panama hat. Rebellious hands, slide down the thighs in the polite manner;

waist, supple waist, bend low—lower yet! Lips, smile ingratiatingly; eyelashes, flutter!

"A lovely morning," I say when the formalities are over. "You're out early, Yamaguchi-san."

"To catch the early worm—forgive me, I mean your husband." Yamaguchi-san titters. "I have a word to say to him."

To gain time I introduce my lodger, and Yamaguchi-san gives him a slap on the back just to show that he knows Western manners.

"Well, how's the old country? How's little old New York?" he cries, for he learned English at business school and has perfected it through his black-market contacts.

"Fine," Sam-san says coolly. It's clear that he doesn't care for this hard-eyed joker.

"As I was saying, I'd like a word with your husband, Nakamura-san." The landlord's voice has changed, his manner with it, like a No actor switching to another mask.

"My husband's in Osaka," I lie quickly. "His boss sent him to buy things for the garage."

"*Sodeska!*" Yamaguchi-san smiles so amiably that I realize he knows what's happened and means to throw us out. He assures me that it doesn't matter, that he'll drop by another day. His errand can wait, he says. (Oh yes, it can wait! Time's on his side.)

"Well, now I gotta be off. Got quite a few visits to make in this neighborhood," Yamaguchi-san says, giving my lodger another slap on the back, harder than the first. "You know, I been aiming to visit your country for quite a while. Biggest country in the world! Japan's too small for me. Well, so long, fella!" he cries, tilting his Panama hat at a still jauntier angle, and he strides off down the garden path.

"A live wire, that," Sam-san says as we stand watching Yamaguchi-san go briskly out through the bamboo gate and then cross the street. "But I'd sure hate to touch a live wire with my bare hands! Guess you feel the same, Yuka-san."

But I am not listening, for I've just learned for sure that I was right. The landlord has stopped to speak to Honda-san, who is about to raise the shutters of her *suchi* shop across the way. He's a real snooper, Yamaguchi-san. No doubt he's asking Honda-san if she has heard the rumors about Fumio, trying to find out also whether I'm behindhand with my bills. That's a favorite trick of our landlord's. In fact he's after Honda-san herself, has raised her rent and wants to force her out of her little shop so as to get on with his building scheme.

"What's the matter, Yuka-san? Why so jumpy?"

I pull myself together and see that Sam-san is watching my fingers twisting and untwisting the belt of my *yukata*. I try to smile at him.

"All right, Yuka-san, I'm not trying to find out anything," Sam-san says. "I'm not like that snake-in-the-grass, landlord-san."

Why do I unload all my troubles on the haro-san? It's not like me, but my too taut nerves are at the breaking point. The feeling that Sam-san is so close to us now loosens my tongue, and I find myself telling him what it really means to be an atom-bomb victim. I explain that we're considered pariahs, bearers of bad luck, and, what's worse, unsuitable for any good jobs. It's true that our poor health makes us undependable as workers. It's true also that our keloid scars are repulsive to look at. . . .

Sam-san puts his hand on my arm (it's the arm on which I have my own scars, hidden under the sleeve of the *yukata*), and says, "Look, why haven't you told me all this before? What's the big idea? Am I a friend or an enemy?"

"I didn't want to bother you with my troubles, Sam-san. You're here on a job—and to see something of Japan. Anyway you're off to Kyoto in a day or two."

"To hell with Kyoto!" he bursts out, but then he grins. "Guess I'm not the type for looking at scenic wonders, temples and all that. Kyoto can wait. How about if I got off a wire to Tokyo and arranged to stay on here a few days longer? The worst my stepfather can do is fire me, and come to think of it, I'd be sort of relieved if he did. By the way, Yuka-san, while I'm about it, I'd better pay you a week's rent in advance."

I look at my lodger without answering. I am overcome with gratitude, but our conventions do not provide me with any words for expressing what I feel.

"Now you go get dressed," Sam-san tells me. "Fumio will be expecting you at the hospital. Should I pick you up there about noon? We'll do the marketing together. Okay?"

I smile my thanks. How settled and secure it all sounds.

"Say, you look about ten years old when you smile!" Sam-san tilts his head, peering at me. "Just about Michiko's age, I'd say! You're as like as two peas in a pod anyhow, did you know that? That's what I was thinking this morning when I came out here and found her staring into that pond. She looks just like Yuka-san, I thought."

"And what was Michiko staring at?" I tease him.

"Well, as far as I could see, she was just looking. Darnedest thing! I'd swear there was nothing there."

I remember the look on my daughter's face as she knelt by the pond at dawn.

"Oh no, you're wrong—quite wrong, Sam-san! There *was* something there. But only Michiko could see it."

Twelve

How lucky that this party for Ohatsu falls in the firefly season! For two nights we've been hunting the hills for fireflies, locking them up in the little bamboo cages that we bring out each spring. As usual, the woods outside town were crowded with people chasing the gaily lit insects, but I'm sure that no one collected as many as our haro-san. The young American puts such zest into everything he does. He is very excited about tonight's party, which Maeda-san is giving for Ohatsu and Hiroo, his star pupil.

"What time do we turn up?" he asks me. "Let's hope the weather stays nice. Do you think I ought to dress up, Yuka-san?"

"No, just run a comb through your hair, for once." I give him a smile, and by now I know him so well that I dare reach up and smooth his always tousled hair. It's as soft as it looks! That soft blond hair of the haro-san sometimes makes him seem just a bit unreal to me.

"Firefly parties begin when the first star comes out," I tell him. "And Maeda-san's pupils will turn up on the dot."

On the dot. There they are in their party kimonos in front of Maeda-san's wicker gate, craning their necks for that first star. It's a rickety house, Maeda-san's, never quite itself since the blast shook it, and one of the young painters giggles behind his paper fan.

"Some day it's going to come crashing down on us in the middle of our painting class! Of course the master would move, if it weren't for the *okasan.*"

Oh, dear. Sam-san fastens on that word *okasan.* (He's set on learning Japanese and is soaking up words like a sponge.)

"Has Maeda-san got a *wife?* You never mentioned her, Yuka-san."

I whisk into the garden, pretending that I haven't heard, hoping against hope that Sam-san won't see Iisa tonight. This is a gay evening, and I don't want to sadden the haro-san with another Hiroshima calamity. But my hopes are quickly shattered.

"Come and greet my wife, my dear friends." Maeda-san welcomes us smilingly. "You must say good evening to Iisa."

His adoration of his beloved wife shines from every feature. Moving softly and signaling his young friends not to let their *getas* clack, Maeda-san leads us toward the garden room, whose outer wall is made of open trelliswork grown over with creepers. A few fireflies have escaped from their cages, and in the greenish light they give we can see just enough of Iisa's room to make out a lacquered screen and her kneeling there. A strange sight: if one didn't know that Maeda-san's wife actually breathes—and eats and sleeps—one might believe that her husband had left a life-sized doll leaning against that screen, a stiff, kimonoed doll which he meant to use as a model.

Quickly I glance at Sam-san. His eyes are half closed
and I seem to hear him draw in his breath. Maeda-san's
pupils are bowing in unison, and Sam-san, looking
about, bows too. All the young men are paying homage to the stricken wife of their master.

I too salute Iisa. I wish I could do more than just in-
cline my body, but words would be of no use. Poor Iisa,
your brain—like the clocks of Hiroshima—stopped
functioning at 8:15 on that far-away August day. My
poor friend! Stunned by the blast, your clothes ripped
off, your sensitive mind gone, you dragged yourself
home—and have not left it since. Your husband found
you nursing your dying baby just inside the gate, with
your eyes fastened in terror on the black atomic rain.

"*Kirei!*"

Kochiro, the youngest of the painters, whispers the
word, "Lovely," and someone else softly repeats it. Of
course! Aren't they all artists, thirsty for beauty? A
firefly has alighted on Iisa's smooth brow, and its lantern casts a sheen over her face. She *is* lovely. Her
hands, patiently crossed in her lap, are as snowy as the
silken folds of her kimono, and her long black hair is

as soft as ribbons of velvet. *Kirei* is the word for our gentle Iisa.

But now the firefly gleaming on her forehead extinguishes its light, and Iisa's face is plunged in darkness. Maeda-san motions us to come away; we mustn't tire his wife. Yet no one wants that poor white doll to feel left out of her own party, so, kneeling on the grass, we sing to her. Our voices little more than whispers, we sing those Hiroshima songs that are so dear to all of us, "When the Black Rain Fell," and "Bouquet in the River." As always, we end with *"Bungaku no ko."* We put our whole hearts into those words, "No more Hiroshimas!" Oh, how close we feel to one another! We are a special species—the radiated species—the only one of its kind on earth. We are brothers and sisters.

"Yuka-san!"

Dear me, I've forgotten the haro-san! The singing has stopped, whispered conversation has taken its place, and I realize suddenly that Sam-san must feel painfully out of things. How rude of me to have neglected an honored guest. I smile at him, feeling guilty.

"Will she—won't she—ever recover?" he asks, and,

like everyone else, he whispers so as not to disturb Iisa. When I shake my head, and then in a few words tell him her story, I see Sam-san's eyes cloud over. He asks me if there are many cases like hers in Hiroshima, and when I nod, Sam-san frowns, looking as he did when Dr. Domoto told him about the various cases in the ward. Yes, Sam-san should have been a doctor. He is sensitive and he cares for life. He must be like his father, whom he talks so much about.

"Re-fresh-ments!" Maeda-san's hoarse voice says the word we've all been longing to hear. "Young people have hearty appetites."

He laughs softly, claps his hands softly. He does everything gently in order not to disturb his wife, and, copying him, we too talk, even *laugh,* in whispers. It's really like a party in a dream. Noiselessly Ohatsu and I move about, carrying platters of *suchi,* of *hishimoshi.* It's such fun serving these young men with their ravenous appetites. They wink at us each time they help themselves to the party food, as rare for them as for us. Between trips to and from the kitchen Ohatsu and I snatch our share, munching those lovely diamond-shaped *hishimoshi* that I baked, and taking quick swallows of lemonade.

When at last everyone has finished, it's my turn to clap my hands. "It's firefly time. Come and get your cages, *dozo*."

Maeda-san's young guests spring to their feet. They kick off their clacking *getas*, so as not to disturb Iisa, before hurrying up to me to get their fireflies. Each of us takes a little bamboo house, whose door we open so that the insects can sail forth. But no sooner is the door open than they mischievously turn off their lights. Fireflies are such teases. One has to shake and shake the cage, and then, just as one is about to give up, they switch on their lights again. "Mine are out!" I cry. And with that our game has started. We all go chasing our insects, giggling, stumbling, softly bumping into one another in the dark.

(Ah, fireflies, fireflies, creatures of spring nights, starry nights! Carrying your own little lamps, you flit and soar, veer and waltz. Those among you who have solitary natures settle on leaves, turning them into sculptured jade in your pale light. Dreamers there are among you. Knowing yourselves to be small, mysterious moons, you yearn toward your elder sister in the sky and, throwing caution to the winds, set your course on her. Tell me, fireflies, do you often faint on your trip to the moon? *Die* in the sky? That's not important. The flight alone is what counts. Yes, yes. Our too-big dreams, our too-difficult journey, are all that counts, fireflies, fireflies!)

The sound of running feet fills Maeda-san's garden. We have all turned into children again, lost in our game, and beneath a tree I bump into Sam-san. He is standing with his bamboo cage in his hand, its door open, and his gaze is fixed on Iisa's hazy figure behind the creepers. He's no longer interested in the fireflies —after all the enthusiasm he put into gathering them. It's as I feared: Iisa's fate is absorbing him, and he can't think of anything else. The party is no party, as far as the haro-san is concerned.

"Come and join us, Sam-san!"

He gives an absent-minded smile, not looking at me. Then to my surprise he puts his long arm about my shoulder, presses me to him for a moment. It's just the way he pressed Michiko to him that morning by the pond.

"It could have happened to *you*, Yuka!" he says gravely.

A wave of happiness that I do not try to explain starts somewhere inside me, gathers force, then sweeps through my whole being. The way he said it and the way he called me just "Yuka" for the first time make me understand that I've come to mean something to Sam-san. I do not move, for I don't want him to take his protective arm away. I want him to feel my warmth, as I feel his, and I say, though without looking up at him, "One thing is certain; nothing bad can happen to me *tonight*."

"Why?"

"Because you're here. That makes me feel safe."

Sam-san's arm about my shoulder tightens, but then he drops it as if he'd remembered that it oughtn't to be there. The laugh he gives seems a little shy. "You know, that's the first time anybody's ever told me that! Gives me a good feeling. I guess it's what every man really wants—to make someone feel safe. Must be part of growing up. Yes, Yuka, it's a funny thing. In a way I've sort of grown up here in Hiroshima—in more ways than one."

Later on all the fireflies go wild, as always happens at firefly parties. They're everywhere—in the trees, on the roof. The irises beside the well look like lit candles because of the fireflies swarming about their tips. The grass has become a luminous carpet, across which stalks Prince Genji, Maeda-san's black cat. His whiskers are silvered with fireflies.

"Elder sister!" I hear a soft voice in the darkness and make out the figure of Ohatsu.

"What is it, small sister?"

Ohatsu hurries up to me, warm and panting from the game. "You're sure you don't mind us having such a lovely time—I mean, with Fumio so sick in the hospital?" she whispers to me. "Elder sister, this is the most beautiful evening of my life! Everything is so beautiful —the fireflies, the stars, the little cakes you made. I'll never forget my party. But—you're sure you don't mind?"

"Of course not, small sister," I answer. "Didn't I tell you that Fumio's getting better? His fever's down and his white blood count has gone up. Now run along to your Hiroo."

"You think that Fumio *will* get well soon, don't you?"

"I know he will," I answer and see the tenseness go out of my sister's face.

"Oh, elder sister, I ache. I love you so much. I love Hiroo so much. I ache with love for the two of you— and I don't know which one I love the most."

"Hiroo, naturally," I tell her, smiling. "Now hurry back to him. That's an order."

Off she flies in her long, clinging kimono. But then she stops, flits back.

"You *promise* that Fumio will get better? You must promise," pleads Ohatsu, and when I answer, "I promise," her eyes light up. She dashes back to the party.

Oh dear fibs, without your help how could I manage? I know that the haro-san doesn't approve of you, but I think he's wrong. Dear fibs, you're so precious—to anyone who loves.

Thirteen

So you've become a father, squirrel. Lucky fellow! Young, healthy, and handsome, you now have sons and daughters peering out of your tree hole, each one a small likeness of yourself. Ohatsu and I brought you a bag of nuts; now you won't have to worry about the groceries. You can sit all day on Fumio's window sill, reminding him and his fellow patients that happiness still exists on our earth. It's strange that men pine for the same things as squirrels—love, health, babies, and peace. But it's easier for squirrels to have those things nowadays than for men.

"Hasn't our squirrel grown fat?" Madoka, the boy without eyelids, asks me from his bed by the window.

Madoka-san's voice sounds wistful. He himself is thin as a sheet of paper; in fact all six patients in the room together wouldn't weigh as much as three healthy men. In spite of this, their bodies bulge in those places where their glands have run riot. Oh, I scarcely dare look at Fumio! Within a short week his arms seem to have shriveled, while his face is swollen to twice its normal size. With the puffed, cracked lips and the tired eyes, my husband's face is like a mask, with "I am pain" the cry that seems to come from its mouth.

"Did you get a little sleep last night, brother-in-law?" Ohatsu asks.

She and Sam-san and I are standing by my husband's bed. He seems to like to have us all close to him. What a strange look there is in Fumio's eyes as he nods to Ohatsu. It's as if he sees more than the rest of us, knows more. What *does* Fumio know? Even if he could tell us, perhaps we couldn't learn from him. My Aunt Matsui says that one must march right up to pain oneself before one can understand its meaning.

Sam-san can't take his gaze off my husband. Each

time he has visited the hospital this week and seen Fumio sinking further, he has stood watching him, his eyes narrowed. Perhaps it's my husband's calm acceptance of his fate that puzzles the haro-san. In his humble way Fumio has climbed to great heights. He has reached a mountaintop where there's no room for the small and the petty.

"Yuka, can I say a few words to Fumio?" Sam-san whispers to me. "Do you mind?"

Sam-san steps closer to the bed. His face is tense as he pushes his hand through that rumpled hair of his. "Look, Fumio, I don't know quite how to put this," he begins. "I'm not much good at saying things. But I want to thank you—I mean, thank you for what you're going through now. You see, it's through you that I've learned the meaning of Hiroshima, and that's something not many people know. I'll tell—a few people. That's all I can do right now—tell people."

Slowly, very carefully, I translate, and when I've finished, Fumio raises his eyes to meet Sam-san's. For a second the two young men look at each other. Oh, my humble little husband, what power has suddenly come into your gaze! Then Fumio smiles—yes, smiles.

The blood rushes into Sam-san's face. Still they keep looking at each other, and for a moment it seems to me that the whole world is standing still—is standing silently with its hat off, bowing deeply to these two young men. The eternal moment passes, but not before it has left its mark on the face of time itself.

"I think Fumio is asleep, elder sister," Ohatsu whispers.

"Yes, small sister."

We move away from the bed on tiptoe. We bow to each of Fumio's fellow patients, then, still bowing, back out into the corridor. And there we almost collide with Dr. Domoto! The ever-cheerful doctor is hurrying down the corridor, trying to keep up with a long-striding Westerner with much hair and a black beard.

"Ha! What pickles I'm in!" cries Dr. Domoto, catching sight of Sam-san. "Please, how's your French?"

Sam-san shakes his head, looking grave. His gangly body is out here in the corridor, it's true, but his thoughts are still in Fumio's room.

"Ah, too bad! All same, come have tea. Come into office," says Dr. Domoto.

[154]

He opens his door, and we all troop in—the Frenchman with the bushy-looking beard, Sam-san, Ohatsu, and I.

"Doctor Bonnard here world authority on genetics and mutations," Dr. Domoto explains to Sam-san. "Alas, my French mostly forgotten, though studied in Paris twenty-five years ago. Doctor Bonnard has come Japan to confer with famous Japanese specialists—Professor Tomaki, Doctor Fujimoto, also Doctor Kikushi, little less famous. Have some pleasant green tea? Yes? Ah, good!"

The tea is being served by a bowlegged little country maid, who giggles behind her hand at the Frenchman's beard. But the Frenchman isn't interested in tea—or in good manners either. He's studying some charts and photographs that lie on the table and, glancing over the top of my cup, I discover that one of them is a picture of a fish. But what a horrid fish!

"Enormously interesting experiment by Professor Tomaki," explains Dr. Domoto, who has cleverly seen that I have been peeking. "Repulsive fish with two heads and four eyes on photo was—"

He looks at me, unable to find the word in English. Then he switches to Japanese. I explain to Sam-san that this fish got irradiated after cobalt rays were put on it in a laboratory. Before long it began showing signs of deformity.

"Yes, yes," Dr. Domoto interrupts me excitedly. "Is right! More cobalt rays, more deformities. After week fish grows two heads, gets four eyes. Same thing may happen to human babies before birth—if mother radiated—or to baby's baby more likely. Mutations skip generation maybe. Person radiated can never be certain great-grandchildren will not look like—like horror-fish."

We crowd around the table, staring down at Professor Tomaki's fish. The Frenchman has a magnifying glass in his hand, and he peers through it a long time, then hands it to Ohatsu with a smile. (Even this black-bearded scientist has been caught by her beauty.) But small sister shakes her head, takes a quick step back. How pale she is! Her frightened eyes steal another glance at the fish, then roam about, as though looking for an escape, and all at once I know I'd better get Ohatsu out of here. I exchange a quick look with Dr.

Domoto. Who is more familiar than he with the ruined nerves and lack of emotional balance of so many of us atom-bomb victims?

"Thank you for paying me visit, Nakamura-san," he tells me hurriedly, taking matters into his own capable hands. "Will see you again soon."

We are out in the street. The sunlight makes Ohatsu look even whiter than she did in the doctor's dark office. Her slender hands are pressed to her breast in that heartbreaking gesture of hers.

"Must run. Have to be on job in ten minutes," she says, although she never knows the time.

I tell her that it's not yet one o'clock and she's not due till two. I'd like to take small sister walking with us, but she insists that she must report an hour earlier today. She flies off. Dear me! I have a flurry of panic and for a second feel like hurrying after her. I never know what Ohatsu may be up to when she's in one of her frantic moods.

"Yuka, stop worrying about Ohatsu. You've got enough worries of your own." Sam-san gives my arm a comforting squeeze. "The kid's in love. She's okay."

I nod and try to make myself believe he's right. But

I know differently. No "kid" who's gone through what Ohatsu has is "okay." I don't intend to tell *that* to the haro-san, though.

We stroll toward the river and cross by the new bridge. Down below we see a little man fishing with a net from the shore, repeatedly drawing in the net from the water and throwing it again. It falls in a circle, sending up a shower of spray. Close by the shore, wedged between two stones, is one of the bouquets, and I hurry on, hoping that Sam-san will not notice it.

"Look, there's a bunch of flowers, just like the other day. It's the damnedest thing! They look just like they'd been put there on purpose."

(Mama-san, I *am* going to tell him now! I shrink from mentioning your too dear name to anyone, you know that, but Sam-san has become one of us now. He must be told. Through him others will learn the things that happened here. So, beloved Mama-san, forgive me if I tell this American boy about your last hours, about your watery Golgotha. Forgive me, Mama-san. *Dozo.*)

"You're right, Sam-san. That's Ohatsu's bouquet,"

I say softly, standing beside Sam-san, looking over the railing.

Sam-san gives a start. "Ohatsu's?"

"Yes," I say. "She puts fresh flowers in the river every morning on her way to work."

And I tell Sam-san what it would have been quite impossible to tell him a few days ago. I've never spoken of it to anyone, not in all these years. I tell him that this was the spot where our mother, become a living torch, jumped into the river after the bomb exploded. The remains of twenty thousand such living torches lie beneath our river, I tell him. And now and then people come to lay flowers on the river's surface. It's the only grave they have to decorate.

Sam-san's hand presses my arm. He doesn't speak; I knew he would not speak. He knows now why Ohatsu snatched those flowers from him the first night he spent in our house.

"Sam-san, I want to tell you about Mama's last moments. I want to tell you, because it's the death that lies ahead of many people, perhaps the end that lies ahead of all of us."

I try to make him see that scene that I remember so clearly, the city of Hiroshima in flames. I tell him about running through the streets that day with my mother and Aunt Matsui, with Ohatsu, a child of three, clinging to my mother's back. Nearly all our clothing had been torn off by the blast; we were almost naked. Fireballs kept shooting through the air, flying jets of flame which consumed everything they touched—trees, houses, and the fleeing people. The streets were so hot that the asphalt bubbled, and many poor dogs were roasted alive because they couldn't get their paws free. I remember how they screamed with fright, those dogs. And Mama must have screamed too, before she jumped into the water. . . .

"Yuka, don't say any more. You don't have the strength."

"I must find the strength. You must know these things," I tell him, "for you're in it now, with the rest of us."

A tree branch fell on me, knocking me unconscious and perhaps saving my life, so I know the end of Mama's story only through my aunt. I tell it now to Sam-san.

"Aunt Matsui says she can't forget the shrieks, can never forget the awful smell of burning flesh. It was she who snatched up Ohatsu from the river bank where Mama had tossed her. Mama gave one cry of despair, then leaped into the water. As she lay there among the others, she turned her beautiful young face toward Ohatsu for one last look. She called out Ohatsu's name before she drowned—at the very spot where you see those flowers. *Her* flowers . . ."

I cannot go on. I cannot. Oh, Mama-san, your blackened face is gazing up at your daughter from the gray water. There is an aureole about your head—your burning hair. I swear, Mama-san, I swear on your blackened face, on your flaming hair, that I will give the rest of my life to prevent such a thing from happening again. Ah, Mama-san, you're smiling at me? Was that what you wanted of your daughter—her promise? Her dedication to the task? Well, you have it. I have made a vow. Now your anguished face has vanished beneath the ripples, and in its place floats Ohatsu's bouquet of flowers. Are you at peace at last, Mama-san? Are you at peace, my darling?

Fourteen

Ko—how shall one explain it, especially to an American? They are as far from understanding *ko*, or from having it complicate their lives, as we are from "kidding" our parents and speaking of our fathers as the "old man." Jolting along on the local train that's taking us to visit Hiroo's family in Kiosoko, I have to smile as I remember my efforts to explain *ko* to Sam-san this morning.

"We don't have anything like that in the States," he said, as if *ko* were a Nipponese specialty, something

[163]

like *sukiyaki.* "I loved my dad, I sure did—but as to filial piety . . ." He laughed. "No, Yuka, I guess I just don't dig this *ko.*"

So then I tried to demonstrate. Snatching up a cushion, I held it to my back and tripped forward, bowing repeatedly. Of course the "baby" kept bobbing forward too.

"I am a Japanese woman greeting her husband. Every time she bows, baby-san bows with her. In that way respect for the head of the family becomes part of him. The beginning of *ko.*"

"Say, Yuka, you're quite an actress!" cried Sam-san.

Encouraged, I shuffled up to him, knelt before him, and made a series of bows so deep that my forehead struck the floor each time.

"Good God! What are you doing way down there?"

"It's the New Year, and I'm thanking my honorable father for all he has done for me during the year. I'm assuring him of my devotion and promising to obey his wishes. That's *ko.*"

But it is clear that Sam-san will never understand, and now as I sit in our rattling train and glance at

Hiroo, seated opposite, I realize that *ko* belongs to us Japanese alone. Hiroo has never questioned it—any more than small sister or I. Because of the solemnity of this occasion—the presentation of his would-be fiancée to his parents—he has put on his formal kimono with the crest of his samurai family embroidered on its wide sleeve. In this attire Hiroo looks quite different, not like a bustling newspaper photographer any longer, but like a figure in one of our classical prints. He holds his handsome body as straight as a sword, and he neither moves nor talks. Perhaps it's just as well that Sam-san didn't come along!

Beside Hiroo, small sister sits peering at the passing landscape, smiling to herself. She's so delighted with our outing that she has forgotten her nervousness over the meeting ahead, which means everything for her future.

"Look, a cow!" she cries. Her adorable nose is flattened against the window. "See that pointed mountain! There's a blue temple!"

Everyone in the compartment is enchanted with Ohatsu, and Hiroo, noticing this, becomes a little less tense. Perhaps his betrothed will make as favorable an impression on his father and mother. How, indeed, could anyone resist Ohatsu?

"Miuchu!" she cries, laughing and clapping her hands as our train pulls into a small station.

"What's so unusual about Miuchu?"

"Nothing. It's only that I'm so happy, elder sister. I just wanted to laugh—that's all."

At the next station, where the train halts for several minutes, Hiroo asks me if I would like some lemonade. I shake my head, for it's obvious that he and Ohatsu are dying to be alone. I spot a stand where souvenirs are being sold—vases carved from bamboo, painted paper fans, good-luck charms—and I leave them and hurry over to it. There I see a tiny cultured pearl shaped like a heart, hanging from a gilded thread, which seems made for my fragile Ohatsu. Though it's only a few *yen*, it's beyond my meager resources. Nevertheless I recklessly buy the trinket and am more than repaid by small sister's ecstatic smile. She clasps her slender hands and whispers, "I'll wear it always, elder sister!"

"It'll bring you luck, my darling."

We have been traveling through rice paddies, but now we leave them and the train chugs through a forest of fir trees, then finally reaches the sea. We run alongside the water for some moments, circling a bay with a wild red cliff facing us on the other side. It's the famous Osima cliff.

"To think that people come here to throw themselves off!" Ohatsu cries, peering out at it with her nose again pressed to the window. "How could anyone be so silly?"

She giggles, just as she did when she looked at the cow and the blue temple. Today everything amuses small sister, even a suicide spot.

"Ah, here we are! Kiosoko," says Hiroo when the train stops at the next station.

He is terribly taut now, and I see a little nerve beating in his temple as we make our way toward his family's house. He's already back in the familiar atmosphere of his home, and no one would guess that on other days he's a Westernized newspaper photographer. For the moment he seems to have forgotten his job, his everyday world—even us. With the expression of someone entering a temple, he passes through the gate and walks stiffly up the path that leads to a modest bamboo house.

A row of cypresses stands before it, and a tiny man and woman, as straight and stiff as the trees, are waiting for us on the steps. Their kimonos are almost threadbare, everything's dilapidated and run down, and yet there's an air of nobility about the house and its owners. Even if I hadn't seen the faded crests on their kimono sleeves, as on Hiroo's, I'd have known that these people were different from Ohatsu and me. Their control of their facial expressions is perfect, their manner of welcoming us charmingly courteous.

"Yoku irashai mashita. Dozo."

When the five of us have finally straightened up from our many deep bows, I sneak a surreptitious glance at our hosts' faces. Dear me! Instead of the prescribed smiles, there is on those gentle countenances a look of distress that startles me. Though their eyes admire Ohatsu's beauty, though I'm sure that they perceive her inner sweetness, something is wrong, terribly wrong. I feel a stab in my heart.

"Please partake of some humble refreshment. *Dozo.*"

We repeat our bows, utter the polite formulas. Then

we kneel in a circle on a delicate straw mat under the
black cypresses, and an aged gnome in a much-darned
kimono pours green tea into bowls as thin as wafers.
The ceremony goes on for a long time, and only polite
commonplaces are spoken. Nothing of importance may
be said at this first meeting between the two families,
but that doesn't prevent the keenest scrutiny from both
sides. What small sister and I *say* means little, but
all-important are the tone of our voices, our pronunciation, our gestures, our expression. Apart from that, our
clothes are discreetly scrutinized. Small sister is finding favor, I know, with Hiroo's parents; indeed, they
seem enchanted with her. But the more they approve,
the sadder become their eyes.

At last I see them exchange a glance. Getting up
from their knees in the graceful manner of gentlefolk,
they address their son, asking him if he will grant them
a moment alone. They are extraordinarily formal with
him as they promise that they won't keep him long or
make him late for his evening assignment in Hiroshima. The responsibilities of one's work come before
all else, says the father gravely, and he bows to Ohatsu
and me and begs us to excuse them for a brief moment.

"Our servant will bring you some fresh tea. Do forgive us. *Dozo*."

"You are certainly forgiven," we answer and bow almost to the ground.

The father, holding himself quite straight, walks into the house ahead of the others. Hiroo goes next, and his mother, moving with that shuffling gait which used to be considered good form for women (pigeon-toeing it, as the irreverent Sam-san would say), follows along three steps behind her son. All is according to etiquette. There isn't a disturbing note, until—

Hiroo turns his head. Oh, dear! The look in his eyes is like that of a prisoner about to be sentenced. Is this really the same Hiroo whom we have known, dashing about in his flannel slacks and leather jacket, carrying his camera, his pockets bulging with film? Are there two Hiroos, then? And are there perhaps two people in every one of us?

Ohatsu has sprung to her feet. "Hiroo," she whispers, and though he can scarcely have heard her, I see Hiroo's tense body quiver. But *ko* instantly takes over. Drawing his glance away, he follows his father into the house. His mother bows her head as she shuffles in after her two masters. Her slender, bent neck expresses a lifetime of obedience and sorrow.

"Elder sister . . ."

Ohatsu's anguished voice reaches me, but I shake my head. I have never before had the courage to say no to one of Ohatsu's appeals for help, but on such an occasion personal feelings must not be allowed to count. Whatever happens, we must act with decorum and in the prescribed fashion. And Ohatsu instantly understands this. Sinking back on her knees, she crouches silently by my side in the correct younger-sister manner.

Thank goodness for the old gnome. He has fallen in love with Ohatsu, as everyone does, and starts pampering her.

"Some tea?" he lisps. "A cake? Two little cakes?"

The gnome beams at my young sister, and Ohatsu bows and accepts a cake. In low voices we exchange remarks on the weather with the aged servant, who tells us that this is the warmest spring in seventy years. (My charming Ohatsu instantly agrees, although she has seen only seventeen of those years.) Trotting on his bare feet, the old man brings Ohatsu a sprig from a cherry tree. He lays his offering before her on the straw mat, instead of thrusting the flowers into her hand, as if Ohatsu were too fragile even to be touched by flowers —she who has been touched by the force of destruction itself!

"Ah, they're coming back, small sister," I whisper.

We bow from our knees as Hiroo and his parents file solemnly from the house. And at this moment I begin to have the feeling that we are acting parts in a play. Just as in one of our ancient No plays, where every constrained gesture, each softly mumbled word, leads to a preordained end, so Ohatsu and I kneel here, awaiting the entrance of the other actors. No dramas often deal with a conflict between love and duty, and so does our drama. But underlying it is a theme more terrifying than any invented by our classical poets. They never conceived of a character doomed to bear tainted offspring—and for this reason forbidden union with the man she loves.

The monstrous fish! I see it reflected in Ohatsu's horrified eyes as she catches sight of Hiroo's face. In her dilated pupils swims that irradiated fish, with its

two lumpy heads and its four unhappy eyes, whose picture we saw in Dr. Domoto's office. I see a shudder
pass through my sister. Does she feel a sudden loathing
for her physical self? Small sister's outer shell is flaw-
less, it is true, but what about the blood coursing
through her delicate veins? Did the wanton bomb
taint for all time the blood and the marrow, and the
womb, of a beautiful girl called Ohatsu?

"Ah, it's already dusk," says Hiroo's father, and it
seems to me that his voice too is like the voice of a No
actor.

"A beautiful evening," I reply.

Can one feel satisfaction in a moment of despair?
The sound of these words, "a beautiful evening,"
which I pronounce in a firm voice, makes me almost
happy. As Ohatsu and I get to our feet, I feel that she
is supported by the strength that emanates from me. I
do not even touch her, yet I know that small sister is
being helped along by me as she crosses the space that
separates us from Hiroo and his parents, her back
straight and her little head high. Yes, I feel I have
enough strength to support us both now.

I embark on the usual formulas for thanking our hosts and taking leave of them, telling them how honored we are to have been received in their home.

"Such a beautiful garden. The view is unforgettable. Thank you so much."

Oh, victory! Victory over myself! That quiet smile which Hiroo's father sends me is like a message of approval. I can see that Hiroo too is satisfied with my behavior and Ohatsu's, although there is a stricken look in his eyes. My heart swells with pride. All by myself I have managed to maintain the decorum that the occasion demands, and thus have lifted the suffering of the five of us onto another plane. I manage one more smile, knowing that at long last I have become a true daughter of Hiroshima.

"We shall have to hurry to catch our train."

"*Sodeska!* You should have a fine return trip. It will be cooler, now that the sun has set. There is a beautiful stretch along the seashore."

"Yes. Very beautiful!"

The expression on the face of Hiroo's father tells me that he has accepted us as kin, even though we shall never be kin. He has accepted us as samurais, even though we are quite ordinary people. He gazes at small sister as he would gaze at his own daughter-in-law.

We begin our final farewells, turning again and again on our way down the path to bow and to smile. As Hiroo draws open the wicker gate, it makes much the same sound as the curtain being rung down at the end of a No drama.

Fifteen

"I have a strawberry for you, Mrs. Bullfinch! The first strawberry of the season."

I slide open the *shojii* and hurry into the house, my plastic shopping bag over my arm. Hurrying's a wonderful habit; it's ever so much better to have your legs run than your thoughts. But once you're in a house, where can you run? I put down my shopping bag and stand listening for sounds that I know I shan't hear. Was it only four days ago that this little house bulged with people, rang with voices? Since Michiko and

Tadeo have been staying with Aunt Matsui, my home has become like a tomb.

I take Mrs. Bullfinch's strawberry over to her cage, and it's clear at once that she's as deep in the dumps as I am. She's perched in her bamboo cage like an old woman, back hunched under her shawl of feathers, head drooping. Her beak is open, and her eyes are half closed.

"Shame on you, Mrs. Bullfinch!" I scold. "Imagine you cat-napping before you've had supper, before I've put the night cover over your house."

But I can't keep it up. I kneel before her cage, and it's with an effort that I hold my own back straight, my own head erect. I'm too tired to get up and brew myself a cup of tea. Still I can't keep my eyes from going to my friendly old china pot in its accustomed place, for this is the hour when I'm used to making tea for myself. Ohatsu must have been thinking of that when she slipped her note under my teapot's fat bottom the afternoon she went away.

"Have gone to Tokyo," she had written there. "Don't try to find me, elder sister. Hiroo insists on marrying me, against his honored parents' wishes, so I must act in this way. I *can't* marry. Every young man has the right to have healthy babbies. My babbies might be like that fish. Elder sister, I love you, but I must disappear. Please forgive me. Respectfully, Small Sister."

Funny, it was Ohatsu's awful mistakes in writing that made my tears start falling. Babbies! Poor small sister never could get her ideograms quite right, and her brushwork was faulty too. As I sat gazing at that sheet of rice paper with a picture of a cherry tree in one corner, it seemed to me that her lopsided characters looked like blossoms that had been scattered by the wind.

But the thought came to me too that that poor ill-written letter of Ohatsu's held a threat of which people had better beware. Ohatsu alone was a weak young girl, but a million—or ten million—Ohatsus would not be weak. If young girls refused to bear children, they would be stronger than the aviators with their bombs. For the aviators had only death to offer, while the "weak" Ohatsus carried in their bodies the seeds of life itself.

"Yuka! Yuka, what's the matter?"

I spring to my feet. My hairpins have dropped out, and my long hair falls about my shoulders. Hours must have passed; it is dark in the room. I am glad of that, for Sam-san can't see my face. But I feel his hand touching my hair, my cheek.

"You've been crying!" I shake my head, but Sam-san knows me well by now, and I can't deceive him. "You haven't heard from Ohatsu yet? That's it, isn't it?"

I nod. Though he hasn't said so, I know that Sam-san believes Ohatsu has taken "the Hiroshima way out." He's heard quite enough about suicides among us bomb survivors to imagine such a fate for my desperate sister. And didn't the classical Ohatsu kill herself for love? Still, I refuse to believe that Sam-san is right and I try not to tremble when I think of the cliff of Osima, which we passed that day on the train. I cling to the hope of seeing small sister again. I'm not going to give up that hope.

Sam-san is scowling. All at once his fist comes down with a bang. "My God, when I think of all the lives that have been ruined by that bomb! Fourteen years since it was dropped, and it's still doing its work. And meanwhile we sit tight and wait for the next one to fall. Well, *I'm* going to do something about it, I'm telling you here and now!"

Sam-san shoves his two hands through his hair. It stands on end like the spines of a furious porcupine. "Yes, sir! I want to *live*. I'm young, and I'm not going to let any push-button general polish me off—not if I can help it, I'm not! Dad always fought for life. Why shouldn't I?"

He breaks off. Someone is calling to me from the garden—or whispering, rather. The voice that drifts in to us is so hoarse, so faint, that I know at once it's Maeda-san. What on earth can he want at this hour?

I leave Sam-san and hurry out into the night. By our bamboo gate stands my old friend, his face looking even paler than usual in the dim gleam of the stone lantern.

"Are you all right, Maeda-san?" I ask worriedly. "And Iisa?"

"Yuka, you must steel yourself. They've just phoned me from the hospital. Fumio—wants you, Yuka," says Maeda-san, and his ruined voice is so low I can scarcely hear him.

[181]

I clutch the sleeve of Maeda-san's kimono, about to ask him what's happened. But then I realize that it's no use. They would never have called me so late at night unless . . . We pass through the gate and begin walking down the street, my steps quickening so that the poor old man has to hurry after me. He loses a *geta*, stoops to pick it up.

"I'll run ahead, Maeda-san," I cry.

"That would be best. I'll catch up with you at the hospital, Yuka. Better hurry!"

Oh, I haven't run so desperately for years! I fly down our pitch-black street and cross the vacant lot to which I bring Nakano-san and Tamura-san every morning. One moment my long hair streams behind me like a sail, the next the wind whips it across my face, half blinding me. I run on and on, out of breath, not seeing where I'm going, stumbling over a board, running on. . . . And suddenly it seems to me that I'm not alone, that around me on all sides are other people, also running, running.

Ah yes, they are the ghosts. Fourteen years ago I ran down these streets with the fleeting throngs. For fourteen years they've kept running inside my head, but tonight they are racing behind me, their faces blackened, their torn skin hanging from their shoulders. I recognize them; they are like people I've seen in a nightmare. That girl with her whole face burned away, that man carrying his wife on his back—they ran by my side that day too. We pass a group of schoolboys kneeling in a circle—all dead. And there's a dog. Ugh! Get out of my way, dog. Your paws are stuck in the melting asphalt? That's what will happen to all of us if we don't run quickly. We'll be roasted alive like you. I can't help you, dog! I must save myself. I must find Mama-san. Far ahead of me I can see the line of the river bank and shadowy forms leaping into the water. Like flaming torches, women with their hair alight hurl themselves from the shore. Is my mother among them? Where, *where* is Mama-san?

"Look out! What's the matter with you, woman?"

I have to grab at a lamp post to keep myself from falling. I've run full tilt into a uniformed policeman, and that brings me back to my senses. I bow and mumble, "Excuse me! Excuse me, please!" then hurry on toward the big bulk of the hospital ahead of me. How well I've got to know it during this last fortnight.

In the hall I catch sight of myself in a strip of a mirror, looking disheveled, wild. Without thinking, I straighten my kimono and arrange my hair. The night watchman walks by, and I stop to bow to him. Then I hurry up the stairs to the radiation ward, bowing again to the night nurse, who is carrying a tray with many little white paper cups. (There's a red pill, no doubt a sleeping pill, in each cup.) Moving on tiptoe so as not to disturb anyone, I reach Fumio's room and softly open the door.

A screen. At six o'clock, when I left here, there was no screen around my husband's bed. Now the nurse has put one up, and instantly I understand what this means. I walk toward it, still on tiptoe, and as I come close I can hear his voice. At first I think there is someone with him.

"Fumio!"

His eyes turn toward me. He can't move his head, but our glances meet across the bed.

"I was speaking to *you*, Yuka," Fumio whispers.

I nod. I kneel on the floor beside the bed, take his hand, and carry it to my lips. His eyes light up as they focus on my face—those sweet, humble eyes of Fumio's that have never expressed bitterness, however roughly life has treated him.

"Yes, I was lying here talking to you," he whispers. "I was telling you all those things I've never said before. I've been too shy; the words never came."

He stops, but I know he has more to say. I wait for him to go on.

"You've been everything to me," I hear Fumio whisper. "You know it, Yuka. I have meant much to you too, and that worries me. I mean, you'll be left with all that love unused and you won't know what to do with it."

I shake my head. He insists, though. "Yes, yes! You see, you've tied up so much love in me, and now that love will all be there—and I won't. What I want to tell you now is—give it away freely. *Everyone* needs you, just as I've needed you. . . ."

He tries to smile, but a spasm of pain twists his face. His whole body contracts. My husband lies there fighting with pain as a man might wrestle with a lion.

I half rise from my knees, meaning to run for the

nurse, but Fumio's emaciated arm moves out to stop
me. He is biting his lips to keep in his cries, not wanting to disturb his fellow patients on the other side of
the screen. (He's so polite; he has always been so polite.) Fumio and the lion lie there struggling together.
I can hear them panting in that terrible life-or-death
embrace.

It's Fumio who wins! I know it when he smiles, and
impulsively I begin to bow. Kneeling on the floor, I
bow and bow to the victor—to the victim and the suf-
ferer—to the great human being who is my husband.
As he sees me paying homage to his suffering and his
triumph, tears form in my husband's eyes, glisten for
a second on his long lashes, then like minute rivers
course through that landscape of agony which once was
a human face. The tears skirt the ridges of his dried
blisters, run over the live sores, make their way into his
open mouth.

"Fumio," I whisper. There's so much to say that I
can say nothing. I can only kneel there, whispering,
"Fumio," and I know that he does not hear me.

He turns his head on the pillow, closes his eyes.

Limply he lies there—so thin, so flat. There's really nothing left of him. What does Fumio look like to-night? Ah yes, my rag doll. My darling rag doll. Oh, Rag Doll, dearest Rag Doll, how much I have loved you all my life.